MIRIAM HEARING SISTER

Miriam Hearing Sister

A Memoir

Miriam Zadek

Gallaudet University Press
Washington, DC

Gallaudet University Press
gupress.gallaudet.edu

Gallaudet University Press is located on the
traditional territories of Nacotchtank and Piscataway.

Printed in the United States of America

ISBN 978-1-954622-09-8 (paperback)
ISBN 978-1-954622-10-4 (ebook)

Library of Congress Cataloging-in-Publication Data

Names: Zadek, Miriam, author.
Title: Miriam hearing sister: a memoir / Miriam Zadek.
Description: Washington, DC: Gallaudet University Press, 2022. | Summary: "The author recounts her experiences growing up in a mixed deaf/hearing Jewish family in New York from the 1930s-onward"—Provided by publisher.
Identifiers: LCCN 2022006609 (print) | LCCN 2022006610 (ebook) | ISBN 9781954622098 (paperback) | ISBN 9781954622104 (ebook)
Subjects: LCSH: Zadek, Miriam. | Deaf—Family relationships—New York (State)—Biography. | Jewish families—New York (State)—Biography.
Classification: LCC HV2534.Z33 A3 2022 (print) | LCC HV2534.Z33 (ebook) | DDC 362.4/2092 [B]—dc23/eng/20220613
LC record available at https://lccn.loc.gov/2022006609
LC ebook record available at https://lccn.loc.gov/2022006610

∞ This paper meets the requirements of ANSI/NISO Z39.48–1992 (Permanence of Paper).

Cover description: Cover image is a blue monochrome photo, depicting a family of five, all white with curly hair, posing in their beachwear. Standing in the back are the father (left) and eldest sister (right). Sitting center is the mother, holding the youngest sister in her lap. Standing to the left is the middle sister, wearing an inflatable tube around her belly. They are all smiling and squinting against the sun. White text overlaid reads Miriam Hearing Sister. Yellow text interspersed reads, Miriam Zadek, A Memoir, Foreword by Philip W. Bravin.

Cover design by Eric C. Wilder.

For my parents
Frances and Hyman Scharfman

If you see what has to be repaired and how to repair it,
then you have found a piece of the world that God has left for you to complete.

—Rabbi Schneerson

CONTENTS

FOREWORD

With the establishment of the first school for the deaf in Hartford, Connecticut in 1817, we saw the development of a definable deaf community in the United States. Today, the deaf community at large is considered to include not only people who are deaf or hard of hearing but hearing family members who have an identity within the deaf community.

In 1929 when memoirist Miriam (née Scharfman) Zadek was born, the only deaf communities consisted of students who attended deaf schools. Elementary education was available, but beyond junior high, schools mostly prepared deaf students to work in manufacturing and trades such as print and machine shops. Postsecondary-level education was limited to approximately seventy-five students per year at Gallaudet College (now University).

The normalization of being deaf was somewhat unthinkable back then. The prevailing belief was that "deafness" was something that needed to be fixed. Deaf people needed to be helped. They needed to be pitied. Such paternalistic thoughts now are neither politically correct nor real.

With the passage of time and increased advocacy, including the passage of the Americans with Disabilities Act in 1990 (P.L. 101-336), limited access to the rest of the world has collapsed. Services such as sign language interpreting, notetaking, and enhanced access to communication through video relay services has led to a paradigm shift. Gallaudet University now has its fourth deaf president after 124 years of only having hearing presidents, there are deaf executives in multiple Fortune 500 companies such as Microsoft and Google, numerous deaf attorneys and physicians, and so much more.

Still, it can be challenging even now for those outside the deaf community to understand that being deaf is merely a biological characteristic that offers access to a rich cultural and linguistic community, not a defect.

***

Miriam Hearing Sister is essentially one hundred years of family drama and achievement. As the middle daughter of a Jewish New York family, Miriam lives half-in and half-out of the deaf world. She portrays her two deaf sisters as fun-loving and capable and especially regards her older sister as a role model. As a child, she sees her family life as unremarkable, no different from other families. During pubescence she is confronted by the terrifying reality of Hitler exterminating the Jews and the "handicapped" throughout World War II. Postwar, she is daunted by dire warnings that come from within her household. Her choices will affect the equilibrium, the life, of the entire family.

Although the story begins in the 1920s and continues through the 2020s, the importance of *Miriam Hearing Sister* is its relevancy today. The presence of deafness holds a critical role for all family members.

***

At the age of ninety-three my aunt Miriam's identity has not changed much. She is still filled with fire and compassion. Through her activism, she continues to push forward the goals of the deaf community—and she looks upon her entire family with pride.

Philip Bravin, '66, former Chair,
Board of Directors, Gallaudet University;
Board of Trustees, Lexington School and Center for the Deaf
Vice President, Product Strategy and Innovation,
ZVRS, a Division of ZP Better Together, LLC

READER'S NOTE

In the chapter "Sisters," Miriam Zadek writes, "In the 1920s, parents of deaf children were faced with competing philosophies, with never the twain to meet. One either adhered to an oral program of lipreading and speech or the use of sign language." For readers who may not be familiar with deaf history or education, the editors of Gallaudet University Press offer this summary.

Formal deaf education in the United States began in the early 1800s. Prior to that, some wealthy families would send their deaf children to schools in Europe to be educated. Deaf children from families of lesser means generally did not attend school. In 1817, the longest continuously running public deaf school in the United States, the American School for the Deaf (ASD) in Hartford, Connecticut, was established by Thomas Hopkins Gallaudet, an American minister, and Laurent Clerc, a French deaf educator. Clerc taught Gallaudet French Sign Language, as well as the manualist methodology for teaching deaf students. Manualists believed that sign language, as the natural language of deaf people, was the most appropriate language for instruction. ASD served as a model for other deaf schools, which began opening around the United States. These schools would also recruit their most successful graduates as teachers, which provided professional employment for deaf people.

In the mid-1800s, oralism—the belief that deaf students should be taught to speak and lipread—gained popularity among educators who taught deaf students in the United States. This led to the opening of oralist schools. One such school, the Lexington School for the Deaf (which was the school that Miriam's sisters attended) was started in 1864 by Hannah and Isaac Rosenfeld. They wanted their deaf daughter to be educated via the oral method and hired a German oralist expert to tutor her and a few other deaf children in their home in New York City. The school quickly outgrew their house and is now the largest deaf school in New York state, although today the school uses both American Sign Language and English to educate students.

In the late nineteenth century, some educators began calling for the establishment of a standardized method for teaching deaf students. In 1880, at the Second International Congress on Education of the Deaf in Milan, Italy, organized and largely attended by oralists, participants passed eight resolutions that declared the "pure oral method" as the superior methodology for educating deaf students.

As a result of the conference, many deaf schools in Europe and the United States abandoned manualism and instead adopted the oral method. Deaf teachers were fired, and signing was forbidden. At the time, many people thought that signing would impede a deaf child's ability to acquire speech. It is now well-known that providing deaf children with access to a natural sign language from birth is beneficial and does not necessarily impede the acquisition of spoken language.

Initially, oralists had won "the war of methods." But, as shown in Miriam's story, sign language persisted in places where deaf people gathered, and continues to be used today.

Suggested Readings

About Us: History. 2019. *Lexington School for the Deaf.* https://www.lexnyc.org/about-us/history.

Baynton, D. C. 2011. *Forbidden Signs: American Culture and the Campaign against Sign Language.* Chicago: The University of Chicago Press.

Cerney, J. 2007. *Deaf Education in America.* Washington, DC: Gallaudet University Press.

Davidson, K., D. Lillo-Martin, and D. Chen Pichler. 2014. Spoken English Language Development among Native Signing Children with Cochlear Implants. *Journal of Deaf Studies and Deaf Education* 19(2): 238–50.

Edwards, R. A. R. *Words Made Flesh: Nineteenth-Century Deaf Education and the Growth of Deaf Culture.* New York: New York University Press.

Hall, M. L., W. C. Hall, and N. K. Caselli. 2019. Deaf Children Need Language, Not (Just) Speech. *First Language* 39(4): 367–95.

History and Cogswell Heritage House. *American School for the Deaf.* https://www.asd-1817.org/about/history--cogswell-heritage-house.

Jowers-Barber, S. 2011. The Complicated History of Deaf Education. *New York Times.* August 1. https://www.nytimes.com/roomfordebate/2011/07/31/do-states-need-schools-for-the-deaf/the-complicated-history-of-deaf-education

Part One

Hearing Voices

SOUND

A deaf house is not a house of silence.
The refrigerator still hums. The furnace motor trips on and off.
Hot water gushes through pipes.
The washing machine slaps clothes with water that reverberates off the sides of the drum.
Radiator pipes not properly bled before winter knock out rhythms.
Then there is the clapping of hands, the stamping of feet.
Sound waves vibrate through air or off floorboards—bypassing the ear but not the body.
"You! Turn around. Look at me. Figure it out! I'm calling you!"

SISTERS

My older sister, Sylvia, was born on March 15, 1923. She was deaf.

Twelve years later, my younger sister, Shirley, was also born deaf on February 22— George Washington's birthday. When she was little, Shirley thought the whole country closed down for *her.* Maybe this contributed to her strong sense of self. Throughout her life, Shirley refused to wear hearing aids, saying, *Everyone knows I'm deaf and knows how to get my attention*. As for the others—*never mind.*

And, then there was me—"Miriam Hearing Sister"—the sister in the middle. The hearing kid. The one who threw off the experts. The sister with whom Shirley and Sylvia had to use speech. The one not to learn sign language because, as Ma said, Shirley and Sylvia had to live in a hearing world. It was okay for them to sign to their friends who were deaf, but the rest of the time . . . Speak. Read lips.

In the 1920s, parents of deaf children were faced with competing philosophies, with never the twain to meet. One either adhered to an oral program of lipreading and speech or the use of sign language. I can still hear my mother's voice saying, "No sign. Speak. They have to live in a hearing world."

HOME

Home was Mount Vernon, New York, a town of 60,000 residents, many of whom took the train each morning to work in New York City. We lived in a small apartment within a tall frame house. Since we lived on the first floor, we had the backyard, and since our apartment was only a fifteen-minute walk to Daddy's store, Daddy walked home every day for lunch.

My school, Lincoln Elementary, was on our street. I walked three houses, waited for the crossing guard to signal, and then entered the school yard. My older sister Sylvia did not go to Lincoln. Each Sunday, we stowed Sylvia's suitcase in the luggage compartment of our black Chrysler 6 sedan and drove her to Lexington School for the Deaf in New York City. Excited to be back at school, Sylvia, her red hair flying, always ran up the steps dragging her suitcase, looking for her friends. Ma and I followed to make sure Sylvia got checked in. After we said goodbye, Ma, Daddy, and I returned to Mount Vernon.

THE BRONX

For me, the treat of our Sunday drive into New York City was stopping at Aunt Molly's apartment in the Bronx before we dropped Sylvia off. Aunt Molly was Ma's younger sister. Her building shared a lot with a small park with a huge outcropping of rock.

Cousin Anne, who at five was a year younger than me but tall for her age, could scale a rock pile like a goat. We spent our time hunting for mica slivers, carefully scaling rocks apart with our fingernails, trying to get the largest, thinnest, most transparent piece of rock through which to view the world. Anne usually made the larger haul. Her skinny arms reached every piece of mica she saw.

Sylvia, uninterested in playing with us little kids, would grab her pile of comic books from the car and go into the apartment. At twelve, she was eager to get back to school, always asking, "How much longer? I want to see my friends."

While Ma visited with Aunt Molly, Daddy stayed in the car. Settling back with a book, he closed out the world by turning off his hearing aid: a boxy transmitter that fit into his shirt pocket and had wires leading to a headband holding the receivers behind his ears.

LEARNING A PRAYER

Cousin Anne knew more prayers than anyone I knew. She had a prayer for eating, another for awakening, and even one for washing her hands. She went to synagogue every Saturday with her father and learned all the prayers of the beginnings and endings of services. Ma tried to keep us observant, but with Daddy working on Saturdays, it was a futile effort. Our family went to synagogue only during the High Holidays.

One Sunday, Anne asked me, "What do you say when you go to bed?"

"Good night?"

"No. What prayer?"

I'd never thought to say a prayer at night. Now that Anne had raised the possibility, it had a certain appeal. "Teach me one," I said.

***

Gute nacht, Shlatn gey
Mlakhin vakh iber mir
tsvey bey meyn kop, tsvey bey meyn his
Tsvey bey meyn linx, tsvey bey meyn rekht
gute nacht

***

Malachan angels, all watching over Anne. I liked that.

Angels watching over *me.*

***

Once Aunt Molly called us into the apartment, she seated herself at the piano and began to play as she sang, "Here she comes. Here she comes . . . Here comes Shirley Temple. Eyes so bright. Steps so light . . . Here is Shirley Temple!"

Anne and I knew the routine. We twirled into the living room as if wearing the short swirly dress worn by Shirley Temple in her most recent movie. Both Anne and I had our hair combed to accent our curls, as was the style back then. Our curls bounced as we danced.

"Again," said Aunt Molly. "You can do better than that."

We waited for the cue. This time we ended our routine with a deep curtsy. Aunt Molly nodded. "Better. Just like Shirley Temple. Just like her."

When it was time to leave, I put my favorite mica pieces into my pocket. We said our goodbyes and climbed into the car. Daddy turned on his hearing aid and we headed into the city to return Sylvia to the Lexington school. I practiced my new prayer all the way there.

UNIFORMS FOR DEAF GIRLS

One Friday when Sylvia came home for the weekend, she told me that she and her classmates were going to force a change at her school. No more skirts or simple blouses. On Sunday, the girls would return to school wearing pants and shirts—just like in the hearing schools.

Signing to Sylvia (I had learned some sign language but never used it in front of our parents), I said, "But we can't wear pants either. All the girls wear skirts or dresses."

"You don't have the same bossiness," said Sylvia. "Not like schools for the deaf. Teacher bosses. Counselor bosses. No more watching everything counselors say—*blah blah blah*— about clothes."

Whispering slowly so that Sylvia could lipread my every word, I explained how things were. "My teacher says, 'It looks neat.' My principal says, 'It's the rule of the school.' My principal says, 'Parents dress up to go to work. Some wear uniforms. School is the business of children. Skirts and blouses or neat dresses are the uniforms of school."

"You don't understand," she responded. "School is like jail. Rules for everything. It's not like hearing schools and living at home, where you are free. This is one rule we will change. It's the only rule we can change. I'm almost thirteen. I have a right to my own mind."

***

The next day Sylvia laid out her plan as we walked to the movies. Thinking out all possibilities, she spoke the entire way. "What can they do?" she asked. "Send a whole class home? How would they get home?"
"Oh, no," I agreed, "they can't send all those kids home!"

Sunday morning, we were in our bedroom when Ma called me. "Tell Sylvia to pack her suitcase."

I stamped on the floor to get Sylvia's attention. "Ma says for you to pack your suitcase."

"Good. Tell me if you hear her coming."

I yelled back to Ma, "She's packing her suitcase."

Sylvia carefully folded her pants and placed them at the bottom. "There," she said, "pants are in."

I touched her shoulder and whispered, "*Shh*! Ma can hear your voice. Stop talking."

Sylvia signaled that she was ready and had finished packing. Dragging her suitcase down the hall and into the living room, she set it near the front door. "Let me open it to make sure you took enough underwear and socks," said Ma.

"I did," said Sylvia. "Five days sleep at school—five days of underwear and socks."

"Open it," Ma demanded. "Open it right now."

Sylvia raised her voice. "*Why?* You don't trust me?"

"Open it!"

Sylvia opened her suitcase. On top were shirts, neatly folded. Beneath were pajamas, socks, and underwear, and carefully rolled beneath those, three pairs of pants. She stared at Ma, defiantly.

"A rule is a rule," Ma said. "No pants means no pants."

Ma took out the offending items and marched to our room. She returned with skirts and blouses to last Sylvia until she came home again.

Sylvia fumed. "If I'm hearing, I wear what I want. No bosses over me at school. No clothes rules . . . No dorm rules . . . I hope the new baby is born deaf. Just like me! Friend for me!"

***

That Sunday we didn't stop at Aunt Molly's. Daddy, staying alert to the traffic, didn't speak. Ma had little to say and didn't look back at us. And Sylvia stared ahead all the way into the city. Emotion contoured her face, but she was quiet as she signed to herself. Her signs were angry and strongly punctuated.

She turned to me. "What if . . . what if all my friends come to school with their pants, and I'm the only one without them?"

At the end of the week, when Sylvia returned home from school, I learned that none of the girls had returned to school with pants.

LET THE BABY HEAR

I knew Ma was pregnant. But babies take a long time to arrive, and there was so much else to think about that I hadn't spent much time thinking about the baby. I thought about what I wanted: a hearing sister to talk to at night after the lights were out. I wanted a live-at-home sister, not a weekend sister. I thought of angels watching over me.

"Let the baby hear," I prayed.

***

One morning not long after my seventh birthday, I awoke to find my parents gone.

"Where is everyone?" I asked.

"Time for the baby to come," said Helen, our housekeeper, who had worked for us for as long as I could remember.

When Daddy returned from the hospital, he was smiling. "It's another girl," he said. "Another sister for you . . . named Shirley." Sylvia was at school. What a surprise for her when she came home for the weekend!

***

Mothers were expected to stay a week in the hospital maternity ward back in these days. But Ma stayed longer. "It's something to do with her blood pressure," Daddy explained. "She'll be home soon."

"Is the baby all right?"

"Fine. Beautiful. Red hair. Healthy."

When Daddy brought Ma and Shirley home, Nurse Ann was with them. Nurse Ann cradled the new baby in her arms as Daddy helped Ma out of the car. I dashed down the steps to hug Ma, then peered into the baby's face—her eyes were tightly shut. She didn't know she was home. "Hi baby. Hi Shirley," I said.

"It's a big day for her," said Nurse Ann. "She's tired."

Nurse Ann had visited over the years. Even after each birth, she came to visit and chat with us. Before joining Ma in the kitchen, she'd greet us with, "Just checking up on my girls." Ann had helped Ma when Sylvia was born and, then again when I was born, when Daddy was at work. But this time was different. She was staying, sleeping on the pull-out sofa in the dining room. She would stay with us until Ma was ready to take over.

WHISTLE

In my dreams I hear that whistle.
It comes from the head of the crib where the baby lies sleeping.
I hadn't known Ma could whistle.
Ma whistles, watches the baby, whistles again.
High-pitched. Steady. One tone.
She whistles, waits, walks away—again and again.
Sometimes while the baby lays on a blanket that covers the floor.
Ma steps up behind, claps her hands.
Once.
Twice.

ANGELS LOOKING OVER ME?

One afternoon, as I sat in my favorite place, a window nook in the hallway outside our apartment, the door to our apartment opened. Daddy and Dr. Kane stepped out into the hallway Daddy looked at the doctor. "Well?"

"She's deaf," he replied. "The baby can't hear. Your wife is right. She can't hear."

I watched Daddy play with the dials of his hearing aid as if a change in volume would change what he'd heard. "But *you* said. . . ."

"We didn't think it would happen again. Look at Miriam . . ." The doctor sounded gruff. "Tell your wife . . . tell Frances we had no way of suspecting. There is no test to predict this. And Miriam. . . . It threw us off. Miriam can hear."

I shrunk back further into the window seat so as not to be seen. What were they saying?

What did the baby's hearing have to do with me?

The doctor opened the outside door, shook Daddy's hand, and promised to come back in a few days "to check on Frances. The baby is healthy. Otherwise."

I sat quietly until Daddy stepped back inside our apartment. I wished I hadn't overheard the conversation.

BECAUSE MIRIAM HEARS

Daddy and Ma began to have long talks before dinner. One evening, now thinking that I had something to do with Shirley being deaf, I stood out of sight, waiting to hear what was said.

"No more doctors," Ma said. "Look at the money we spent when Sylvia was born. We went from doctor to doctor until Dr. Kane told us that nothing would change, that we should save that money to educate her."

"They told us the baby would hear," said Daddy. "Like Miriam—because Miriam is hearing."

Because Miriam is hearing. My toes curled tight onto the doorway threshold.

Then Ma said, "I hear voices."

"Voices?" Daddy sounded puzzled. I imagine him fiddling with his hearing aid, pushing the volume button back and forth.

"Voices," said Ma. "I'll be walking down the street and I'll hear someone call my name. I turn around and there's no one there."

"It's nerves. You'll calm down, and then the voices will stop. It's been too much."

"The doctor says I should go away for a while. I can't go away. Who will take care of the baby? And the girls are in school."

"We'll manage," said Daddy. "We'll manage."

UNLEARNING A PRAYER

What had happened to the angels? Maybe I'd learned the prayer Anne taught me in the wrong language. Maybe my angels didn't speak Yiddish. Maybe the prayer should have been said like this:

Good night. Now I'm going to sleep
Angels will watch over me
Two at my head, two at my feet
Two at my left and two at my right
Two overhead, all around me
Good night

The words in English didn't sound as soft. Nor was the prayer as easily whispered. I didn't feel the same warm blanket of protection and safety.

Soon I stopped saying the prayer.

DADDY'S STORE AND THE WORLD OF FOURTH AVENUE

Daddy was known around town as Mr. H. I., short for Mr. Hyman Irving Scharfman. Ornamented with a giant neon sign that spelled out its name, The Fair Store—possibly the largest along Fourth Avenue—offered four floors of retail shopping space. Upon entering, the first thing anyone saw was a large sign centered inside its entryway: SATISFIED CUSTOMERS BUILT THE FAIR.

The salespeople were specialists who made window shades; measured carpeting; and equipped kitchens with dishes, glassware, pots, and pans. Dolly was the expert on the main floor. Born and raised in Mount Vernon, she knew everyone and had no trouble remembering china patterns or pieces of glassware that customers wanted or had in their homes.

During the Great Depression, running such an enterprise as The Fair Store was an exercise in survival. To support our family and keep employees on the payroll, Daddy put in twelve- to sixteen-hour days, with Ma helping out, especially during holidays.

To speak with Mr. H.I., the salespeople knew to face him so that he could see and hear them. They adopted this same strategy for communicating with Sylvia. As longtime employees, they had known Sylvia and me since our infancy. I'd learned to ride a tricycle in front of The Fair Store. Now they would be watching baby Shirley grow up, too.

***

No question about it—our lives revolved around Mount Vernon's shopping district. Fourth Avenue was where Ma bought her clothes from the Bromley Shop and the Letty Lee, and where we shopped for new shoes. The Bee Hive Restaurant was where Daddy treated us to ice cream sodas. We carried home butter ladled by the pound from large tubs and wrapped to go in waxed paper from the Bon Ton Dairy. We ordered our monogrammed paper and later our wedding invitations from the Barish Stationery Store.

But, at age seven, I used the pocket change Daddy gave me to buy potato chips and pretzels at the five-and-ten cent stores. And I bought a tiny skirt and shirt similar to mine so that baby Shirley and I could dress alike as sisters.

DADDY'S CIRCLE OF LIGHT

After dinner, Daddy would sit in his easy chair, light the living room lamp, open the book on his lap and turn off his hearing aid. Not a sound could intrude. Only when we touched him on the arm—startled him—did he look up.

As I grew older and more aware, I saw how Daddy moved from his circle of light, his books, from us to Ma. I saw how they engaged each other. As I grew older, I didn't always agree with their joint decision-making, though I did understand that any decision that came from one came from both.

This stayed with me, how families work. How solutions can be developed in a collaborative way.

MOMMY OR ME?

The morning Grandma Bessie arrived in her big black sedan to meet the new baby would become one of the most memorable days of my life. Grandma had been driven to Mount Vernon from her home in Jamaica, Long Island, by one of "the boys," which was what our entire family called her five tall sons.

I'd helped Ma set the table for lunch knowing exactly what she'd serve: a platter of fresh vegetables with slices of tomato herring in the center, another platter of rye and pumpernickel breads. And, as always, marble cake for dessert.

As everyone gathered at the table, I saw nothing different. I told myself, *Everything is going to be all right. Nothing has changed. This visit is just like any other—only now another deaf kid in our family.*

But, I wondered, *did Grandma know that Shirley was deaf? Did my uncles know? Did they know that Ma was hearing voices?*

Whenever family visited, a trip to Daddy's store was a must. Everyone wanted to see the store's newest merchandise and do some personal shopping. Daddy's store provided dishes, carpeting, window coverings, and cookware for all the relatives.

After lunch, after Grandma had held Shirley and nodded in approval, we went to Daddy's store. Sylvia, as usual, was away at school, and Shirley stayed home with Nurse Ann.

After briefly chatting with Daddy, Grandma began to walk around the store, noting new items since her last visit. I was on my way to the basement level where all sorts of things—clothespins, clips, screws, small washcloths, bottle corks, twine, linoleum squares, fancy ceramic tiles—could be made into toys. On each visit I took home a collection to make cloth dolls or a clothespin doll family, or for lining a dollhouse floor.

As I stood on the landing, Daddy came over, bent down his head, and spoke in a low voice. "Miriam," he said. "Miriam, if Mommy and I didn't live together, who would you want to live with? Your mother or me?"

"Oh, I'd live with you," I said, hardly understanding what this would mean.

Daddy hugged me. I walked down the stairs to the basement. Wandering aisle to aisle, looking at notions, fingering my favorites, I thought about what Daddy had asked. What had he meant when he said . . . *if he and Ma didn't live together?*

I didn't know anyone whose parents didn't live together. Only old people lived alone, usually when someone had died. If not together with Daddy, where would Ma live? Where would Daddy live? And where would that leave Sylvia and Shirley and me? What if Daddy asked Sylvia what he had asked me? What would Sylvia say? And what about Shirley? She was too young to make a choice.

I didn't want to make a choice. If Ma had asked me the same question, I'd have given the same answer: "With you." Then they would have to keep living together because I wanted to be with both of them.

I decided to tell Sylvia to say the same thing if they asked her.

BREAKDOWN

It all happened so fast. There wasn't time to tell Sylvia anything. Ma came to my school, collected reports on my work, and found out what subjects my class would study for the rest of that semester. We were going to Florida.

When Sylvia came home for the weekend, she was full of questions. "Why Florida? No deaf school?"

I didn't know the answers. One day Ma and Daddy were talking about the baby and then, suddenly, we were on our way south so that Ma could recover from her nervous breakdown.

And that's how Ma always referred to it afterward.

"Do you remember when I had a nervous breakdown, and we went to Florida? . . . Remember what the doctor said? How he would have told any other person, 'You must spend time in a sanatorium.' But not me. He knew how strong I was. He told me, 'Get away for a while and when you get back, you'll be able to do what has to be done."

Ma always added, "He had faith in me. He saw what a strong person I was. He knew I'd adjust and do the right thing."

SISTERS DIVIDED

Two of us would go with Ma and one of us would stay with Daddy. I didn't know why. And I didn't know what a breakdown was. I felt frightened and Sylvia was of no help.

How could I tell Sylvia that having another deaf baby was causing Ma to hear voices? How could I explain that it was because of me—the one who could hear—that baby Shirley was born deaf? I didn't understand it.

Ma could hear. And if Daddy's hearing aids were turned on, and you faced him as you spoke, Daddy could hear.

Although Sylvia was deaf, she and I could understand each other. The only hard part of having a sister who couldn't hear was that she didn't live at home during the week like my friends' sisters.

Sure. I wanted the new baby to hear. But if Shirley turned out to be as much fun as Sylvia, then maybe everything would turn out all right.

ON THE ROAD

Daddy took us to Florida. The trunk of the Chrysler was packed with our summer clothes. Sylvia and I added our bathing suits, our roller skates, our books, and our games. Ma added pots and pans and other kitchen items. When it came time to say goodbye, Nurse Ann stood on the porch with Shirley in her arms, repeating, "Just relax. Enjoy yourself. I'll take good care of the baby. She'll be fine."

Sylvia and I hugged Nurse Ann and Shirley. Then we climbed into the car with books, paper, pencils, and crayons for the long ride. The car's front seat was a long bench that easily held the driver and two passengers. Ma sat in front with Daddy. Uncle Sam, one of Ma's younger brothers, scooted in. Uncle Sam had taken time off from his business in New York to help Daddy drive to Florida and back.

Sylvia and I gazed out the car windows for hours as we followed our way down on the map we'd spread between us on the seat. Passing through town after town, inches became miles. Each time Daddy stopped for gas, Sylvia and I ran to the shack where you paid. Oil companies supplied gas stations with roadmaps promoting the oil company's name. Roadmaps were free to customers.

Each time we stopped, Sylvia and I rifled through the map display. We collected maps for each state and while many seemed to look the same, Sylvia and I held the hope that one might contain a detail our other maps did not.

As we started to accumulate maps for places we wouldn't visit, Daddy drew the line. "Now look, girls," he said, "you've got maps all over the back seat. You do not need maps for the Midwest. We are not going to the Midwest. So, no more maps. No more clutter in the back seat."

INCHES TO MILES

Outside our car, we sometimes saw shanties along the tracks. Early morning and after school, we'd see children playing in their yards, and we waved to them. Sometimes the children waved back.

But our road trip to Florida was most remarkable for the roadside signs sharing jingles. A first sign might offer only three words, but the jingle completed itself within the next four or five signs waiting for us in the distance.

I'd nudge Sylvia and point. "There's another one." She'd nod and begin to scribble the words onto a pad.

THROUGHOUT THIS WORLD
OF SORROW AND SIN
YOUR HEAD GROWS BALD
BUT NOT YOUR CHIN
BURMA SHAVE

In the front seat, the grown-ups chatted about business and family, with Ma and Uncle Sam repeating old stories about life on the Lower East Side, like how Grandma had come to school one day with a cup of milk in her hand because Uncle Sam had not finished his milk at lunchtime. In front of his entire class, he had to drink his milk, hand the cup back to Grandma, and return to his seat in the classroom.

"Sylvia, do you know about Grandma and the milk?" I asked.

"What milk?"

I explained.

"Never knew that story," she answered. "Same bossiness . . . just like Ma."

That's true, I thought. Or, maybe, that was still true. Nothing seemed different about Ma. She looked the same. She talked with Uncle Sam and Daddy the same. She laughed the same.

Maybe the voices had gone away. Maybe it could happen that fast—or maybe not. I just didn't know. Was Ma still hearing voices? Was she hearing people calling her name? Were imaginary people calling her name? Were they calling her, only her?

"Ma," I said. "Ma . . ."

"What now?" she asked.

"Nothing . . ."

Finally, I asked Sylvia what she knew about breakdowns.

"Breakdown?" she asked, making the sign for broken. "Ma broken?"

"No," I said. "She hears someone calling her, but, when she turns around, no one is there."

Sylvia grinned. "She should be deaf, like me. Never hear someone calling you."

I giggled.

***

Unless Ma had something to say to us, she never turned to see us in the back seat. Well, if we asked her something, then she had to turn. Ma couldn't understand Sylvia unless she was watching Sylvia's face and when Ma spoke, Sylvia had to lipread.

Sometimes, Ma didn't bother. She'd tell me to "tell Sylvia."

Except for gas or meals or to sleep late at night, we never stopped. As the weather grew warm, we lunched at roadside stands—corn was sold at some and warm tomatoes at others. Some stands advertised animal parks, much to our eagerness. But the animals turned out to be poor old animals who just lay there. Wanting souvenirs to remind us of this trip, Sylvia and I searched for something to buy. But there was nothing we liked.

We stuck with our maps.

***

The farther south we drove, the more abundant the Spanish moss. Swaying in the breeze, it looked like tightly woven lace hanging from the trees in ragged curtains. When the tree branches met over the narrow road, the lace enclosed us, shutting out the light. I was beguiled.

"Stop, please," I begged. "Let me touch and take some of the moss."

"No moss in the car," said Daddy, and Ma and Uncle Sam agreed.

"But it's so beautiful."

"It may look beautiful out there on the trees," said Ma, "but it's probably full of bugs."

FLORIDA

This was Florida. We saw orchards hanging with fruit. We saw signs advertising oranges and coconuts. We saw our first palm trees.

Outside an Indian village, we saw coconut shells carved with faces.

Sylvia and I begged to stop. "Maybe another time," said Daddy. Again, Ma and Uncle Sam agreed. The closer we got to Miami, the greater their hurry. *Maybe when we go home.* I asked, "Ma, we are going home sometime, aren't we?"

"What kind of question is *that*? Of course, we are going home," she said. "In a while. First vacation and a new school for you and Sylvia. Then we'll talk about going home."

"But I don't understand," I said. "Why is Daddy going back to Mount Vernon? Why isn't he staying here with us?"

"Because," said Daddy, "I have to run the business, and I have to help Ann take care of Shirley."

SWIMMING POOL

Our small apartment in Florida faced a central courtyard with a swimming pool and lounge chairs clustered under large umbrellas to shield bathers from the sun's rays. We had one bedroom and a sleeper sofa in the living room. The tiny kitchen was big enough for our daily meals.

Daddy and Uncle Sam helped us get settled. Before they left, they stocked the kitchen, placing staples on the closet floor when the kitchen's limited shelf space could hold no more.

"It's different from home," I said to Sylvia.

As my older sister hurried to open her suitcase and pull out her bathing suit, she nodded. "Yeah, no swimming pool in the backyard at home."

"No swimming yet," said Ma. "Not while there's no lifeguard."

"But I'm a good swimmer," insisted Sylvia, as she demonstrated the breaststroke.

Ma spoke straight into her face. "No lifeguard. No swimming. Look . . . as soon as we put everything away, we'll go outside and then you can swim."

Sylvia turned back to me and said, "And *she* doesn't even know *how* to swim."

ALL IS WELL

Daddy called once a week, and Ma would ask about the baby.

He'd say, "She's fine. Growing and looking around."

During one call, Daddy reported that Shirley was "lifting her head." That she was "Alert. So alert . . . Notices everything. The nurse says she's never seen such an alert baby."

"Good," said Ma. "Good. Maybe she'll be a good lipreader. Like Sylvia."

Daddy must have asked about Sylvia and me because I heard Ma tell him how we were spending our days. I wanted to talk to him myself, but Ma said it was awfully expensive to make a phone call from so far away. She said, "I'm letting Daddy know that all is well."

All is well. I remembered that.

SCHOOL UNDER THE UMBRELLAS

Ma enrolled Sylvia and me in the same school. And Sylvia was right: There were no other deaf students. Our new school wasn't really like a school at all. It was a big old house with chairs and patio tables with umbrellas arranged on the lawn.

On our first day, Ma explained us to the teachers. "When you talk to Sylvia, she must be looking directly at you. Speak slowly and clearly, and she will understand you."

The teachers seemed uncertain. One said, "We've never had a deaf student."

"She's a good lipreader," said Ma. "Her work for the school term is outlined in the papers from her school. Sylvia is capable of doing whatever is required. You will see. If there is any problem, just let me know. Or ask Miriam. Miriam understands Sylvia."

The teachers looked from Ma to Sylvia. Sylvia's eyes were fixed on Ma's lips. Ma was continuing to explain that Sylvia was just like every other kid. *Just like every other kid—only smarter.* So long as you remembered not to talk with your back turned to her, to stamp on the floor to get her attention, to touch her shoulder when you wanted her to turn to face you.

They'll see, I thought.

***

The teachers had shiny new workbooks for us. We didn't have to write our answers on separate sheets of paper. We did arithmetic sums with the teacher checking our work. We wrote short sentences and stories on other pages. Then we went to a room that served as the school library and borrowed books.

Just as we did work assignments from our schools at home, all the other kids were working on the same assignments as their classmates at home because all the kids were there on vacation. Like us.

On sunny days, we sat outside together at tables with large umbrellas.

"No one deaf here," said Sylvia. But she'd already made friends with hearing kids. They'd learned the rules. They tapped her arm when they wanted to get her attention and looked at her as they spoke.

BACK TO NORMAL

We vacationed in Florida for two months. Then one day on our walk to school, Ma said, "We need to get your reports to give to your teachers at home."

It was time to leave. Ma had stopped hearing voices.

We repacked our suitcases. This time with souvenirs—shells we'd gathered from the beach—and copies of assignments to show our teachers at home—and, of course, our workbooks, our very own workbooks to show our friends. Because there would be no kosher food on a northbound train, Ma packed the food for our trip home.

We forgot to take the maps. The maps we left behind to gather dust on the bookshelf were likely discarded by the next tenant.

We rode the train from Miami to New York City. As the train sped through the small towns, stopping only at the bigger cities, Sylvia and I worked on our knitting. Throughout the night I heard noises: the calls of conductors, the loading of mail crates, the whistle of the train as we rounded curves in the track. By daylight, we saw the same shanties we'd seen on our trip south. Children waved from their yards. Adults looked up as they hung lines of laundry to dry in the wind of passing trains.

When we arrived at Penn Station, Daddy was waiting. Nurse Ann held baby Shirley—red hair, big brown eyes.

"My girls are home," smiled Daddy. "All my girls."

Daddy put his arm around Ma, and she reached for the baby. "Well," she said, "you did a good job, Ann. She looks fine." She turned the baby's face. "Hello. Hello there. Hello, Shirley."

Our lives went back to normal. I walked to Lincoln Elementary School. Sylvia spent weekdays at Lexington School in New York City.

And Ma no longer talked about hearing voices.

THE QUESTION

It was after our return from Florida that I saw our neighbor the lawyer.

I'd adjusted my roller skates and hung the key attached to an old shoelace around my neck. I skated down the sidewalk, around the corner and back, free-coasting and jumping over uneven patches of concrete. When I wanted to slow down or stop, I stepped on a grassy plot.

The lawyer came outside to greet me before I'd skated past his house. "How is the family?" he asked.

"Fine, thank you."

"And the new baby?" Because it was a small town and an even smaller neighborhood, families knew each other.

"She's adorable," I said. "Red hair and she turns over and lifts her head and . . ."

"Do they know if she is deaf?"

"I don't think she hears," I said, "but . . ."

The lawyer stepped closer and spoke in a quiet, confidential way. "Tell me, Miriam, do they know what causes the deafness?"

"Well," I said, "maybe she fell off the bed and bumped her ears . . ." I knew that was foolish. Did anybody fall off the bed and bump their ears?

He raised his eyebrows. Then, as he turned to go back inside his house, he said, "Give my regards to your parents."

I wasn't about to give Ma and Daddy the lawyer's regards. What if they asked what more had been said? Except for Sylvia, all the other people in our family could hear. No deaf cousins, uncles, or aunts. Even Daddy could hear with his hearing aids. Was Shirley deaf because I could hear?

I skated home, past the lawyer's house, past those houses with the older couples who had no children for me to play with. Reaching our driveway, I headed toward the back door and into the kitchen. Ma was cleaning the stove.

"Ma . . ."

"What?"

"Why are Shirley and Sylvia deaf?"

Ma stood straight, stretched her back, turned to me.

"We don't know," she answered. "Miriam, we just don't know. Even the doctors were surprised. They don't know why either."

NO ANSWER

Sylvia did almost everything better than anyone I knew. She could hit a ball farther than anyone. She'd taught me to roller skate. She was the one who organized the kickball games on our street.

Her sports trophies stood on the dresser. I picked up each to carefully examine it. When Sylvia was home on weekends, I wasn't allowed to touch her treasures. In the next room, Shirley was in her crib making noises. I peeked in. She lifted her head and looked at me. "Ma," I called, "can I pick up the baby?"

Ma's muffled "Yes" came from the kitchen, followed by "Practice your clarinet lesson."

Nobody knew why Shirley and Sylvia didn't hear. They just didn't know. That was the story I would grow up with.

I carried Shirley to my room and laid her on the bed. Taking my clarinet from the closet, I assembled it and placed my new sheet music on the music stand. It was a bright, thumping piece I needed to learn for the spring parade with the school band. I tapped my foot and started to play. Shirley watched as my fingers pressed the levers. I played the piece again and again until I could play it perfectly. She never cried.

"Someday," I said to her, "someday, you'll stand outside when I walk by with the band. I'll see you and you'll see me, and we'll say, 'That's my sister!'"

Part Two

Before Ma Had Daughters

EARPIECE

The squeal interrupted
Pulling the hearing aid out of his ear
Daddy checked its connections
Took the battery pack out of
His pocket. misshapen by weight,
Fixed and lifted the earpiece up
Pressed it into his ear canal
Turned to me, expectant
And I began again
Our conversation

BEFORE MA HAD DAUGHTERS

Ma told me how Daddy had lost his hearing and how she'd discovered that Sylvia couldn't hear. I already knew how Ma had discovered that Shirley was also deaf; I'd been there as Ma whistled and clapped.

But first things first. Ma's parents had come to the United States from Europe. They'd settled in on the city's Lower East Side where Ma and her six siblings were born and raised.

By 1921, Ma was working as a bookkeeper for a New York City law firm. In the evenings, she helped her father in his small grocery and notions store on Houston Street.

The first time Daddy saw Ma, she was restocking her father's shelves. Daddy's cousin owned the shop next door. As a young boy, Daddy had emigrated from a *shtetl,* a small Jewish town in Russia, to the Lower East Side with his four siblings and widowed mother. By the time Daddy met Ma, who was twenty, he was in his late twenties and already owned his first store. The Fair Store came after he married Ma.

Ma spoke of Daddy's persistence in courting her. He took her for rides in one of the neighborhood's only cars but always with one of her brothers. To hear her describe Uncle Moe made me shriek with laughter. Only a boy then, Moe was put in charge of cranking the car to restart its engine.

Within a year, Ma and Daddy had married. Returning from their wedding ceremony at a catering hall near Ma's home, Ma's neighbors lined the sidewalk to cheer the newly wedded couple.

Sylvia—a sturdy, active, red-haired baby—was born one year later. Sylvia seemed just like every other healthy baby until one morning. When Ma saw that Sylvia didn't turn at a sound that had alerted her friend's child, Ma started clapping her hands, banging pans, speaking in a loud voice until she realized that nothing—*nothing*—got a response from Sylvia.

To get Sylvia's attention, the source of the sound had to be within sight.

Ma's hearing was acute. So, without a known history in either Ma or Daddy's family, it was assumed that Sylvia being deaf was connected to Daddy.

***

Several years before Daddy met Ma, he'd fallen ill with the flu. Within two years' time, the Spanish Flu had infected about a third of the world's population and killed 675,000 Americans.

Daddy remembered waking up in the hospital with his mother leaning over his bed, moving her lips as if speaking to him. He described how he'd looked up and asked why she wasn't using her voice. "Speak up," he'd said. "Why are you whispering? I cannot hear what you are saying. Speak up."

Then the frantic inquiries. "When will he get his strength back? When can he leave the hospital? Will his hearing return when he recovers?"

Immigrants from immigrant neighborhoods waited at bedsides. Relatives, cowed by white-garbed doctors and nurses, leaned close to understand words and medical terms and struggled to translate them into their own native languages. Finally, it was left to the children to convey what might be understood.

"He's alive," doctors said, loath to repeat in Yiddish what could be understood by Grandma, who was still clinging to the language of her homeland of Russia.

"Be thankful," said the doctors. "So many have died. He's alive."

When the specialist arrived, also wearing white and impatient to move from patient to patient, he concurred. "Nothing can be done." Back home, away from the doctors and nurses in their white uniforms, away from the stretchers rolling down hallways, away from the rattle of hospital trays and coughing patients, away from the sickness, the family continued to ask, "Will he hear again?"

Then the realization. No straw of hope left to grasp.

THE DOCTOR HEARS, BUT . . .

My friend Margie lived only six blocks away. When I rode over on my new bike, which I got for my ninth birthday, she was waiting outside. "Can I ride?" she asked.

After a couple of tries, she got her balance and off she rode and back again. We took turns all afternoon on my two-wheeler. As it got late, I got on for one more ride. Feeling secure, I didn't pay attention to the hole in the sidewalk that we'd been avoiding all afternoon.

The bike hit the hole and fell, with the handlebar landing on my leg. "Ouch!" I cried. "I can't stand." Lifting the bike, Margie pulled me up. Leaning on her shoulder, I hopped up the steps into her apartment.

Margie's mother said, "As soon as I'm done with Stuart, we'll call your mother."

Stuart was Margie's little brother and the same age as Shirley. He'd begun to speak in short sentences. Now speaking to us from his potty, Stuart turned to watch me hop around—and out came a stream of pee. Margie and I burst into giggles, and Margie's mother giggled too. Not knowing he was the cause, Stuart looked delighted.

***

At home that evening, Dr. Kane, the doctor Ma always called, insisted I walk down the hall. I started, then refused. "It hurts too much."

"Hm. Then I'll come back tomorrow, and we'll try again."

I became a champion hopper as, day after day, Dr. Kane arrived at our house to insist that I walk. When Ma was finally tired of this, the doctor said to meet him at the x-ray center in his office building. Daddy came home from work and drove us.

Once I'd stretched out on the table with the x-ray machine centered over my lower leg, the technician took a picture.

"She's fractured a bone," Dr. Kane said. "The tibia. She'll need a cast for five weeks...I have patients waiting in my office. Bring her back later. In the meantime, I'll wrap a magazine on her leg."

Ma glared at Dr. Kane before saying, "She has gone almost a week with a broken leg, with you insisting that she could walk. There will be no coming back later. There will be no magazine. There will be a cast. *Now*!"

Without another word, Dr. Kane stepped to the equipment closet and took out wrap and plaster and a pair of crutches. He applied the plaster to my leg and checked to see that the crutches were the appropriate length.

"The cast should stay on for five weeks," he said. "Make an appointment for me to remove it."

***

Shirley, now two-and-a-half, was fascinated by the plaster cast. She rubbed it and punched it. Looking into my face, she raised her eyebrows, as if to ask, "What is it?"

I used a sign I thought meant "broken," but that didn't do it. How to explain? Maybe Sylvia could explain it.

When Sylvia came home for the weekend, "Clumsy!" was the way she defined it.

***

Dr. Kane's plaster cutters looked like the big scissors Daddy used to trim tree branches.

"You're going to use those on my leg?" I asked.

Dr. Kane smiled. "Yes," he said, "but I usually don't cut off the leg."

As the doctor cut through the plaster, he chatted with Ma. He shared that he'd just given a new fur coat to his wife and discussed her growing collection of rings.

Later that night Ma said to Daddy, "I guess we just bought another jewel for Dr. Kane's wife."

***

Without the cast, my leg looked skinny and white. My limp lasted a long time. "Why is she still limping?" asked Ma.

"Just give it time," said Dr. Kane.

Ma took me to the Hospital for Ruptured and Crippled in New York City. I knew I wasn't crippled, but I was afraid to ask what ruptured meant. Doctors told Ma not to worry.

Eventually, my limp did disappear—as did my bike.

FIRST CLASSROOM

Friday nights
Shabbos dinner
silver candlestick
five candles
one for each
Ma said
as she lit the candles
and said the prayer
Daddy blessed the wine and
the challah

Saturdays
the candlestick moved
to the sideboard
Shabbos cloth, table mats
to the closet
out came Shirley's notebook

SHIRLEY'S LESSONS

On each and every Saturday, Shirley attended lessons at our dining room table. Until Shirley was three years old, old enough to be enrolled in the Lexington school day program, a succession of teachers came to our table with briefcases stocked with paste and crayons and pages to put in loose-leaf binders.

The previous Saturday's lesson—pictures of everyday items cut from magazines and pasted onto blank pages—was spread out and waiting. Vocabulary words had emerged from these pictures for Shirley to learn, to lipread, to *speak.* Unlike my friend Margie's little brother, my little sister was learning sounds through finger and lip movements in order to master a language she couldn't hear.

When Shirley's shoulders slumped, the teacher said, "Watch . . . watch." And Shirley watched. When Shirley's attention drifted—when her eyes strayed to the window, to the living room, to the hall—the teacher placed a hand on Shirley's chin and turned her face back toward the teacher.

When Shirley simply refused to be pushed into imitating the voice she didn't hear, she shook her head and said, "No," a word she'd quickly learned. Red corkscrew curls bouncing, she gestured *No* by shaking her head and looking away. Sometimes, Shirley started a race. She dashed around the table, knowing better than to try to escape out the door.

Ma hovered in the hallway. To support the teacher, Ma had suggestions. Perhaps a short break, a treat as a reward, anything to keep Shirley trying to imitate sounds.

Sometimes Sylvia stood and observed. "I hated speech lessons," she said. "Hated when they put their hands on my face . . . and tried to force me to look.

"Shirley will learn someday. They can't force you to look if you close your eyes."

MISS MAGNA'S SCHOOL OF THE DANCE

As soon as we became old enough, Ma enrolled us as students at Miss Magna's School of the Dance.

Once a week, pushing Shirley in her stroller, Ma walked us to Miss Magna's two-story brick house. The entryway was dark. To our right, what had been a long, rectangular parlor was now a mirrored studio with a piano and ballet barre.

How I wished to be on my toes at that barre. But there would be no pastel tutus or dainty ribbon-tied slippers for me. No arabesque. No plié. Ma thought ballet dancers looked foolish, especially when the dancers were spindly-legged girls who didn't flesh out their tunics.

At least that's what she said.

Tap dancing was a different story. It was fast-paced and exciting. At least once a year we went into New York City to see the Rockettes at Radio City Music Hall. Tap dancing had a discernible rhythm. Between the pounding of the piano and the vibrations of the taps striking the floor, it was quite difficult to miss the beat.

***

We wore patent leather shoes, one ribbon tied across the instep, silver taps peeking upward heel and toe—and practiced in shorts and shirts. Flashy, bright-colored tap-dancing costumes were worn only on recital day.

For practice clothes, the ballet students wore tutus from previous recitals and ballet shoes in pastel colors with ribbons crisscrossed and tied around their ankles. Girls on pointe knew what to do with skinny arms like mine. Elbows were tucked against the body and forearms gracefully rested on the tutu. As my elementary school friends stretched and posed, turned, and leaped, they smiled in my direction.

***

Because Sylvia's lesson came first, I learned her routines before my own. Each sequence ended the same way. *Brush, brush, down—first with the left foot leading, then the right. Step, step, close.*

Miss Magna performed new routines mirror-style so that Sylvia could read her lips. But once she'd introduced the new step, she turned her back to Sylvia. Then, like a dancer with a shadow—a shadow that sometimes missed a beat—Miss Magna and Sylvia danced in unison.

We'd been tap dancing for two years when Sylvia decided it was time to quit. Ma insisted she complete the lessons and appear in that year's recital.

"There will be time for boys and friends later," Ma told Sylvia.

***

The dance recital program listed Miss Magna's dancers in order of appearance. Groups of younger children performed first. Sylvia's solo performance was midway.

"Sylvia keeps the beat by paying attention to the vibrations from the piano," explained Miss Magna, as if the novelty of a deaf tap dancer would spark even greater anticipation for the afternoon's full program of dancers. "Now we present to you Sylvia Scharfman in 'The Dance of the Wooden Soldier.'"

Applause.

As befit a wooden soldier, Sylvia held her body erect—shoulders straight, arms stiffly in position. The audience members knew the music. Mothers of the more advanced students even knew the steps. By the time Sylvia began tapping her way to her routine's conclusion, the applause started anew.

Miss Magna stood off stage in the wings. Modeling for Sylvia that she had the audience in the palm of her hand, Miss Magna bent forward straight from the waist. *Bow.*

Prompted each time by Miss Magna, Sylvia bowed and bowed again to the dark.

NO WORRIES

By the time Shirley turned three, she was my little shadow. With me as her assistant, her favorite activity became acrobatics. An older lady, who lived on the third floor of the house that overlooked our yard, waved and clapped at Shirley's somersaults, handstands, and cartwheels.

One day, Shirley had a new act. She made a sweeping gesture with her arms. *Round.* She wanted me to grab her by the legs—and with her arms spread like the wings of an airplane—she wanted me to spin her *round and round.*

I grabbed her legs. Tightly held her ankles. Slowly, I began to turn. As I spun faster and faster, she shouted with glee. I felt myself becoming dizzy and out of control, and I staggered across the yard. My arms gave out. *Thump!* Shirley's head hit the ground.

I let go. Shirley scrambled to her feet. Holding her head and crying, she ran to the back door.

"What happened?" asked Ma. "Why is she crying?"

"We were turning, spinning," I gasped, "and I got dizzy. Her head hit the grass."

"A bump," said Ma as she examined Shirley, grabbed a washcloth, wrapped some ice in it, and pressed it against Shirley's head. "A bump right near her ear."

Forgetting that Shirley wasn't watching my lips, I asked, "Better? Better?" She couldn't know I was talking, but her crying stopped.

Had that bump made her deaf? No. She was already deaf. Would that bump make her even more deaf?

Because doctors had said, "Just one of those things that Sylvia is deaf. . . . No need to worry. Miriam hears. . . . No need to worry." Because I could hear, Ma and Daddy hadn't expected to have another deaf child.

Or was Shirley deaf because I could hear?

A ROOM OF MY OWN?

One evening Daddy came home with news. Our landlord Mr. Mellis had bought and renovated another house just two blocks away on North Fulton Avenue.

"The house has three apartments," Daddy told Ma. "The first-floor apartment has three bedrooms, and he's interested to know whether we'd like to move there."

"But," I cried, "my friends are here!"

"Enough," said Ma. "Your friends can walk to you, and you can walk to play with them." She turned to Daddy. "We do need more room. It's crowded here. Sylvia is bringing friends home on weekends, and it's time Shirley moved out of our bedroom. Call Mellis and tell him we'd like to see the place."

Daddy got up from the table, pulled his hearing aid receiver out of his shirt pocket, held it to the phone, and dialed our landlord. Arrangements were made. When Ma and Daddy went to see the apartment, I went with them. It was just a 10-minute walk.

The house was larger. The first-floor apartment had a third bedroom—not a whole room but a large alcove off the second bedroom. "I want that room!" I said. "I want privacy. . . . I want Shirley out of my stuff."

"Okay, okay," said Ma. "During the week you can have that bedroom all to yourself. On weekends, when Sylvia comes home from school, you'll sleep in the other room with Shirley."

And that's the way it went. From Sunday evening until Friday afternoon, I had my own room.

THE BIG BACKYARD

When I told my friends Diana and Louie that I was moving, they had a big surprise for me. "Guess what?! We're moving too!"

That summer we moved into the same house. My family moved into the first-floor apartment. Diana and her brother Louie, who was two years older, moved with their parents into the third-floor apartment. And how fortunate for me, because when Diana's mom sewed broomstick skirts for Diana, she made skirts for me too. When Louie designed paper-doll dresses for Diana, he gave me duplicates.

The new house had a much bigger backyard, with a chestnut tree, a garage, and an empty lot behind. Borrowing from the Sunday comics, Diana and I pretended to be Flash Gordon and Dale. With her flowing, long blond hair, Diana was Dale. Hours of combing did nothing to straighten my auburn curls. When there was nothing better for Louie to do than hang around with us, he did. When I complained of boredom, they said in unison, "Go count your freckles!"

Life was good. We built a long tent in the backyard by throwing old sheets across the clothesline and pegging the sheets to the ground with twigs. We piled pillows, blankets, dolls, games, and little Shirley and her baby carriage into the tent with us and, when more space was needed, we hung another sheet.

For that first summer together in our new apartment house, we were happy to spend time playing only with each other.

NEIGHBOR TO THE LEFT

Mrs. Grossman's house, which was made of stone and pillars, loomed over us. Some days, as she wandered around her backyard, Mrs. Grossman stood at the hedge looking into our backyard. She was our neighbor to the left. Her side of the hedge was bordered by beds of roses tended by a gardener. The gardener also kept her lawn. Mrs. Grossman wore sweaters and skirts, while our mothers, unless they had somewhere special to go, wore simple house dresses.

"Imagine her nerve," said Ma, "saying she felt so sorry for you—that you had to play with Shirley all the time. Some nerve! Shirley is my responsibility, not yours. I decide when you help. You do no more than other children."

It had all started the day Mrs. Grossman invited me to play with her kids.

"I can't," I said. "I have to watch Shirley today."

"I understand," she said. "We all understand. So much responsibility." She turned to the friend beside her. "This is the little girl with two deaf sisters."

NEIGHBOR TO THE RIGHT

Mrs. Jamison, tall with white hair, lived on the right side of our house. She was always pulling her gardening gloves on and off. She hired no gardeners to do her work; it was her pleasure.

She had terraced her garden into three levels of plant life: flowers, vines, and vegetables. Showing interest in Shirley and me, she pointed out new growth and offered us freshly picked vegetables. She invited Shirley to walk with her between the rows. Shirley went willingly and was always permitted to choose and pick a flower.

Then, one morning, Mrs. Jamison gestured to keep Shirley away. "It's polio," she told Ma.

***

That summer, Mrs. Jamison's house was very quiet, despite the fact that her son and his wife, and their two children, too young to be of interest to us, were occupying its second floor. She pointed toward their windows. "The children . . . both of them," she said, "have polio. You know, infantile paralysis. They can't move their legs." We listened with dismay. "And across the street, it's the worst kind. The boy has bulbar polio and he's having trouble breathing."

That boy lay in an iron lung with air forced in and out of his lungs. That didn't help, and he died.

Ma called the doctor and he told her, "Don't let the girls go to the movies or to places that are crowded. Call me if anyone gets a cold or runs a fever or develops achiness in an arm or a leg or has problems moving. There's nothing more to do but wait."

Meanwhile, newspaper headlines reported polio outbreaks across the world. News photos showed an Australian nurse, Sister Kenny, binding the limp, thin limbs of her patients with hot woolen wrappings, using a special treatment she developed.

The shape of summer had changed. Diana and Louie were sent to visit a relative. No friends came to our house to play. Parents were concerned about a neighborhood block with three reported cases of polio.

Since we were not allowed to go anywhere, we sat on our porch or played together in our backyard. We checked to be sure we could still move our arms and legs. Trying not to seem too curious, we watched whenever the visiting nurse paid a call on the children next door.

TRICK OR TREAT

The kids next door slowly got better. Once they had recovered, we were encouraged to play with them but to never ask about their polio. "It's easier for them if you don't," said Ma. "It's too upsetting to talk about." Diana and Louie's mom told them the same thing.

Polio was something you did not talk about. So, because we never asked questions, we never found out what it was like to wake up unable to move your legs or arms. We were also left to wonder what it might feel like to have your arms and legs wrapped in hot woolen cloths.

Autumn brought an end to that summer's epidemic, and we all started going to school again. On Halloween that year, Daddy brought home a small, perfect pumpkin for Shirley. She proudly carried it throughout the house. She rolled it around the backyard and carefully wiped it clean so that nothing matted to its sleek orange surface. She placed it in her carriage and pushed it around to the front step.

A cry that rose to a wail caused me to come racing just as the boy from next door jumped off our front step and ran down the sidewalk.

There at Shirley's feet was her pumpkin, smashed to bits. Tears streamed down her freckled cheeks, making large wet spots on her shirt. "Pumpkin. . . . Break pumpkin."

I knew what had happened. "She couldn't even hear you sneak up, you dumb jerk! Polio didn't make you any nicer!"

I had not cried when I'd learned Shirley was deaf. I did not cry when I wondered what Ma's nervous breakdown meant. But now, all because of a stupid pumpkin, I cried and cried.

HOLY SMOKES

"Wait 'til you see what I have," said Sylvia. She signaled me to follow her to our bedroom, where she placed her suitcase on the bed and pulled out her clothes.

"Wait," she said. "Wait. I need to put the clothes in the laundry hamper." She ran down the hall to the bathroom, arms loaded. When she came back, she closed our bedroom door behind her.

"Look," she said. "Look at this." She pulled out a package of tubular pasta. Next, she reached into a corner of her suitcase and pulled out a book of matches.

I'm sure my eyes must have widened. "Matches! What are you doing with matches?"

"Can Ma hear you?"

"I don't think so. She's giving Shirley a bath."

"Come on," said Sylvia.

We left our bedroom and walked to the back door. The matches were hidden in the palm of Sylvia's hand and the box of rigatoni against her chest. She didn't turn around to see if I was following. She knew.

Once we'd slipped inside the garage, Sylvia beckoned me over, and we ducked down alongside the car. She took two pieces of long, hollow rigatoni out of the package and handed one to me. Sticking the end of a piece in her mouth, she gestured for me to do the same. Then she took the matchbook and tore out a match. Lighting the match and holding its flame to her pasta, she lit its end. Then she held the burning match toward me.

"Now breathe in," she commanded.

I did. I coughed. I gasped, "We're smoking."

"That's right. But not cigarettes."

Match after match she lit. Rigatoni does not stay lit easily. I never heard Ma come into the garage until it was too late.

Ma shouted, "What are you doing?" though she saw us standing there, match lit, trying to create a cigarette from a piece of pasta.

"How dare you play with matches. And what is *that* you're trying to smoke?" Ma grabbed the rigatoni package from Sylvia's hand. Knowing how angry Ma was, Sylvia ran out of the garage and down the driveway.

I ran toward the kitchen, Ma chasing me. I ran toward the sink and found myself trapped, wedged between the sink and the stove. Ma came right up to me. *Slap!* against my arm. *Slap!* across my cheek. I started to cry.

"Don't you ever let me find you doing that again," she fumed. "Never. No playing with matches! And you'll really get it if I find you trying to *smoke* again. Go to your room."

Sobbing, I ran down the hall to my bedroom and threw myself onto the bed. Where was Sylvia? About fifteen minutes later she walked into the room.

"What happened?" Sylvia asked.

"Ma hit me," I cried. "I got caught in the kitchen between the sink and the stove and I couldn't run."

Sylvia shook her head. "Sometimes," she said, "sometimes, you are stupid. You don't use your head. When Ma gets angry, just get out of her way. Give her a chance to get over it. I never get hit because I go the other direction. Don't know how you get along when I'm at school."

I didn't know either.

CONEY ISLAND SUMMERS

Ma felt ocean air and sunshine carried big benefits for our health. And by summering at Coney Island, we avoided all sorts of wintertime ills.

Ma called our three-room Coney Island apartment "choice," and our relatives agreed. Our apartment fronted the ocean and though it was separated from the sand, balcony stairs led under the boardwalk to the beach.

On weekends, much of Long Island emptied onto the Coney Island beach. That hot, crowded subway ride from Jamaica, Brooklyn, and points farther north was worth it. Our building, the Jefferson Baths, even had a separate area for day-trippers who rented lockers by the day and could enjoy a steam room and showers.

Lunchtimes were on the sand where we spread our old blankets from home. Ma spooned large portions of spaghetti onto paper plates. As we dug in with mismatched forks from the apartment, the plates dampened and lost their shape. Once we'd emptied our lemonade and iced tea jars, we made sure to carefully stack our waxed paper cups for later use, while we threw away the paper plates.

Hawkers sold snacks on the beach. Those without a vending license were at high risk. An officer could confiscate their ice chests and snacks as well as impose fines and ruin their day's livelihood.

Whenever a hawker sought protection, my cousins and I were quick to throw a blanket or towel over his chest of ice cream and potato knishes. The hawker looked just like another family member—at least for the time it took the officer to walk away down the beach. In return, he was likely to reach into his ice chest and offer us ice cream sandwiches.

MY SWIMMING BUDDY

Ma and our adult relatives were certain that swimming right after eating would cause you to flounder and require rescuing. We cousins waited impatiently for the half-hour rule to pass as we kept asking the time. More than anything, we wanted to jump back into the waves.

Because I was not as strong a swimmer as my older sister and cousins, Ma relied on Sylvia to be my swimming buddy whether we got into the water after lunch or in the mornings before the family arrived. Every morning before breakfast, even before the lifeguards came on duty, our Coney Island adventures started with the two of us pulling on our bathing suits, grabbing our towels, and heading to the beach for a quick swim.

Jumping into the surf, the waves hit our bodies. With saltwater stinging our eyes, we pushed our salty strands of curly, stiffening, red hair away from our faces. Crawling back onto the beach, we shook off the sand and wrapped ourselves in towels before running to shower.

I think it was because Sylvia was such a good swimmer and so competent at everything that not one of us stopped to think: If Miriam gets into trouble, Sylvia won't hear her cries for help.

HOW MA'S HAIR TURNED WHITE

One summer, Ma told the story of how her hair turned white. All the aunts and uncles nodded in agreement because they'd seen it happen before I was born.

One morning when Ma and Sylvia were vacationing at Coney Island, Ma walked down the street and into the corner grocery. Grocery list in hand, she thought Sylvia was right beside her. But when Ma looked down—*No Sylvia*!

Ma rushed out of the store and scanned the main thoroughfare and the side street. No red-haired kid in shorts and white sandals. No kid in sight.

If Sylvia had headed back to the apartment, she'd need to cross that street. She'd need to go through the entryway to the apartment building, and climb the steps to the balconies. She'd need to walk the lengths of those balconies to find, among dozens of identical doors, the door to our apartment. Ma ran to the Jefferson Baths.

The grocery store owner called the police. Within minutes, Coney Island police units were notified of a lost child: *Three years old. Red hair. Named Sylvia. Will not respond to name. Unable to provide information. Deaf.*

Fears were that adventuresome, beach-loving Sylvia might wander into the ocean. Lifeguards set to combing the shoreline. Summer neighbors joined the search. Daddy came from Mount Vernon. Within hours, relatives arrived from Brooklyn and Jamaica.

The day wore on with no sign of Sylvia.

By evening the entire family was in deep despair. How do you search the dark for a child who cannot hear you calling her name?

***

At 2:00 a.m. the next morning, a man walked into the police station with a bedraggled, red-haired child. When the police asked her name, the little girl didn't answer.

The man, a Luna Amusement Park ticket taker, said the girl had shown up early at the carousel, and he'd thought her parents would come looking. In the meantime, between collecting tickets, he'd treated her to carousel rides and fed her ice cream, hot dogs, and sodas. When the park closed for the night, he brought the girl to the police station.

They all had been alerted about her disappearance and immediately knew that this was Sylvia. Police officers gave Sylvia candy, put her in a patrol car, and drove her home. Though the Jefferson Baths Apartments were located many blocks away from Luna Park, the amusement park was in a straight line from our apartment.

"And the next morning," said Ma, "I woke up and my hair was white."

***

For years, my cousins and I—who'd only ever known Ma's hair to be white—believed every word of what Ma said. But as time went on, and we heard other stories of traumatizing events, we realized that Ma's stories often concluded in this same way:

"And that was when my hair turned white."

Part Three

Just Like the Princesses in England

MIRIAM HEARING SISTER

As I grew up, I had many monikers. At each stage of life, I acquired another, each replacing the last. All were derived from my given name, Miriam, but the one that stuck longest was given to me by my sisters and their deaf friends. They voiced it and they said it in sign: "Miriam Hearing Sister."

As sisters, we had secret ways of communicating, always attuned to subtle body language as much as to Ma's well-practiced techniques, like stomping the floor to get attention. Because of this and our attempts to integrate sign fragments with lipreading, we understood each other. Between us, there were no hard parts to "hearing."

So, it was natural, from the age of seven, when my thirteen-year-old sister and I shared a Florida classroom, that I would help. As I'd listened to Ma speak with the Florida teachers, I'd wondered, *Hadn't they ever met a deaf kid before?* Not using my voice, so only Sylvia could follow, I'd said, "It's okay. Just me helping if they think you won't understand. But you will. Smart." We nodded in agreement.

Back home in Mount Vernon, I happily became my teenage sister's connection to the outside world. I made her telephone calls; back then, none of the relay services we have today existed. This worked when a hearing person was present to answer my call and could convey Sylvia's message to a deaf friend.

Sylvia didn't want Ma to make calls for her. "I don't want parents butting in. I want my privacy," she said to me. "You know to keep secrets. Right?"

I nodded. "Right."

"I'll make my own plans," she said, "then tell Ma when she can't change them."

"I keep good secrets. Never tell Ma!"

She patted me on the shoulder and pointed me to the phone. I pulled the wall phone into the hall closet. Sylvia raised her eyebrows.

"Because then Ma does not hear me talk." I crawled in amid the boots and coat hems to sit on the floor. Sylvia sat next to me as I made the calls.

241ST STREET STATION

By the time Sylvia turned sixteen, Daddy had stopped driving her to school on Sundays. Instead, we drove to the 241st Street Subway Station so that Sylvia could catch the Lexington Avenue Express. From there she returned to school on the train with her school friends.

Each Sunday, Sylvia faced off in the kitchen with Ma and Daddy. She'd cajole, beg, and nag to leave early to meet her school friends at the station. Lexington was an all-girls school after its first few grades. The girls had a ritual early meeting time, which was primarily for the purpose of connecting with the boys heading back to the New York School for the Deaf, known as Fanwood, in White Plains.

Daddy's standard response was, "It's your mother's decision."

And Ma would shake her head at Sylvia and say, "What kind of place is that to meet boys? Whoever heard of meeting boys at the subway station? If the boys want to see you, then they can come to the house."

Sylvia's eyes flashed. "How do they get here?" she asked. "How are they going to get here when they have to go back to school?"

"You saw your friends last evening at the party in the Bronx," said Ma. "Why do you have to run back now? Wasn't that enough?"

Sylvia glanced at me. Her curly red hair looked like it might stand on end. "You don't tell Miriam that she can't see her friends. She gets to walk up the street or call them on the phone. Tell me about deaf kids in Mount Vernon. None! I have no deaf friends here It's not my fault I was born deaf."

That did it. That always did it. Sylvia had made her case.

"Then Miriam goes along," said Ma. "When you get on the train, Miriam will call us, and we'll pick her up."

Every Sunday it was the same. Never mind that the buses always picked up the boys at the same time. Never mind that Sylvia had classmates who'd board the train with her. Never mind that Sylvia was sixteen and I was ten. Sylvia was not to risk waiting alone at the station—not for one moment. Daddy and Ma needed to know she'd gotten on the train and was safely on her way back to school. Sylvia rolled her eyes at the impossible demands of our parents but grudgingly accepted. She understood that if she didn't, her chances of socializing were greatly diminished.

"Remember," said Sylvia as we raced to our room to get ready, "you won't act silly."

"I *never* act silly."

"And no interruptions when we sign."

"I won't."

"And you won't tell Ma any of our secrets or plans. It's *my* business."

I promised. "Never will tell."

***

We got into Daddy's car, and he drove us past the town center, deserted on Sunday afternoons, to where the sleepy suburb of Mount Vernon adjoined the apartments of the more populous Bronx. There, at that boundary, was the 241st Street subway station, the social capital of Sylvia's young life.

Daddy turned to face us in the backseat. "Now remember. Miriam, you call as soon as the boys board their buses. . . . I won't have your mother worry. And, if the buses are late, well, you call us and let us know."

Bouncing out of the backseat of Daddy's Chrysler, we ran up the station steps. Sylvia took me by the arm to propel me faster.

THE ROAR OF THE TRAIN

By the time the train arrived at the subway station it was above ground, having traveled through the suburbs on an elevated track.

Sylvia could not hear the roar of the train as it arrived, nor the hiss of its brakes or the clap of its metal doors slamming open. Neither could most of her school friends. But everyone could feel the station's floor vibrate.

Few passengers rode to this end of the line. Those who did walked through the corridor from the train's platform, pushed through the turnstiles leading to the ticket area, and walked down the steps to the street. But the boys on their way to the White Plains school piled their suitcases in a corner next to the girls' suitcases and leaned against the station's heavily embossed iron grillwork and dusty windows between the ticket booth and the far corner of the entryway. The few other passengers leaving or arriving at the station glanced in our direction, likely intrigued by the chatter in sign language.

This interlude between trains and buses allowed for a review of the past weekend's parties and the opportunity to make plans for the next. It was the only way to keep in touch without having a hearing relative call.

At 4:30, the school bus arrived for the boys, and we emptied the waiting area. We watched as the boys climbed aboard the bus, opened windows, and sent final messages back and forth with their fingers.

Sylvia's friends turned to me, hugs going round before signing, "See you next week!"

Sylvia signed, "Remember," and gestured zipping her lips.

I signed back, "Never tell." Her secrets were safe with me.

The girlfriends pushed their coins into turnstile slots, lugged their suitcases onto the subway platform, and turned to wave goodbye to me again. I went downstairs to the phone booth for Daddy to come to get me.

NOT FOR YOU!

Sylvia's ticket to the station was the presence of her little sister and her friends knew this. They also knew I was willing to make phone calls for them. Even the boys noted my presence. In greeting, Sylvia signed, "Miriam, hearing sister." Arms embraced my shoulder in welcome.

A dark, slim teenager named Salvatore, a recent recruit to this gathering, always arrived mid-afternoon. I watched for him as each train discharged its passengers. When he arrived, he swiftly engaged the group, waving to boys he knew from school and joining in the conversation, but only after smiling at me, patting my arm, and signing, "Hello."

I limited myself to "Hi." By Sylvia's instruction, I was to stand there, smile, be pleasant and not interrupt. Able to understand only fragments of what he signed, I had to get my clues from his voice.

I noticed that Salvatore always wore a sailor's cap. So I'd worn one too. And Salvatore noticed. He touched my cap, touched his cap, and signed "Same." I wore that cap all that next week. Finally, I told Sylvia.

"Too old for you," she said. "Not for you. He's deaf."

I put the cap away. Occasionally I found myself staring up into my closet, taking down the cap, and trying it on. Ma didn't understand why I'd been so insistent on buying it. And I thought, maybe when I turn sixteen, I'll wear it again. Not at the 241st Street station but at high school. Yes. That's what I'd do. I'd wear my cap to a gathering of hearing boys and girls.

MY AUTOGRAPH BOOK

Forget me not
Always be #
Always be u
Never be flat
Love,
Marjorie
Class 6 – 2B

In June 1940 we carried our autograph books everywhere. We were the oldest and tallest students at Lincoln Elementary School. It was time to graduate.

During our last week at Lincoln, we practiced marching into the auditorium and across the stage every morning. The two sixth-grade classes walked down the halls in a straight line, turned right toward the auditorium doors, and waited for the two boys in front to hold open the doors as the rest of us walked to the front where Mrs. Swan and Mrs. Meyer stood.

They looked at us and whispered to each other in their quiet teacher voices. Finally, one said, "Stand according to height." We shuffled positions, giggling as we measured girl against girl, boy against boy. "Now, two by two, get in line . . . shortest in front, please." Mrs. Swan went to the upright piano, played a chord, and signaled us to slowly walk down the aisle with a partner in time to the music.

Two boys marched from the back of the auditorium. One carried the American flag and the other the State flag. They solemnly walked to the stage, and we stood to recite the Pledge of Allegiance.

Once the boys had placed the flags in the flag holders, they took their seats, and it was our turn to walk across the stage, demonstrating that we knew how to take our diplomas in our left hand, which freed our right hand to shake the hand of our principal.

I asked Margie, "What if I mix up the hands?"

"Just think: Diploma and left are in the front of the alphabet. Principal and right are on the other end."

"Huh?"

Rehearsal ended with our singing of "The Star-Spangled Banner" and "God Bless America." When the flag bearers brought the flags down from the stage, we followed them, two by two, out of the auditorium.

***

From my autograph book:

My dear sister,

How lucky are we? Do you know why? Because we will be graduated at the same time. You are still younger to go to another school but I have to go for trade. Boo boo for trade. Don't forget about our old times and quarrels.

Try to be good sisters.

Love, Sylvia Sally

I'd be moving on to seventh grade at William Wilson Junior High just as Sylvia completed eighth grade at Lexington School for the Deaf and moved up to the school's vocational division where sewing and other domestic arts were offered. Being deaf wasn't thought of as an obstacle in the semi-skilled trades. Sylvia was seventeen and wanted to go to work in a factory.

GRADE SCHOOL GRADUATION: JUNE 22, 1940

Germany's defeat of France would overshadow my graduation from Lincoln. Germany had already invaded Poland, Netherlands, and Scandinavia, and news of the spreading war had become routine. Gabriel Heatter's nightly wartime commentaries filled our kitchen as Daddy stood holding his hearing aid receiver against the radio. When the French government signed an armistice agreement with Germany just two days before my graduation, this, somehow, made the Second World War seem closer to home.

My classmates' preoccupation with the war was evident. To reach our graduation ceremony in the auditorium, our parents walked through a corridor that was an exhibit of our war poems, essays, and art works, including drawings and paintings of battle scenes we'd seen at the movies.

Following the ceremony, my family went to the Bee Hive Restaurant, which was across the street from Daddy's store. Its most memorable feature was its long, narrow lunch counter with chrome stools topped with red leather seats that spun around. One minute you'd face the counter, the next you'd face people walking to the dining area. But it was graduation day, a special day, so we sat in a booth.

"Well, Girl Graduate," said Daddy, "now you are ready for junior high school."

"Daddy, what will it be like walking to school if we have a war? What will happen if there is a bombing and we're at school? Junior high isn't just up the block. . . . It's almost a mile away."

"We're far from Europe. We're across the Atlantic," said Daddy. "It's not a worry,"

"You're sure?"

***

From my autograph book:

To Miriam,
First you learned the piano

Then the clarinet
If you decide to play the drums
Call on me, I have a set.
Your Uncle Mike

Dear Miriam,
Remember that knowledge is power
and that you are most apt to succeed.
Your loving cousin (from Newark), Martin

To my loving niece,
Don't wait for your ship to come in
Row out and meet it.
Love,
Your Uncle Eddie

To Miriam,
To see her is to love her
And only her forever
For nature made her what she is
And nevermore another.
Your Uncle Sam

***

None of us could foresee that within a year all the cousins and all the uncles—the uncles I so loved for always telling a story to make me laugh—would be serving in the US Army.

HOW DO YOU GET SCARED?

Sunday, December 7, 1941. Bundled in snow jackets, mittens, and scarves, Cousin Anne and I sat on her stoop in the Bronx as Aunt Molly and Ma visited.

Then Ma came outside. "Get Daddy," she said. "Right now. Tell him to come into the house."

That cold day, Daddy had stayed in the car, as usual. Turning off his hearing aids, glasses sliding down his nose, he'd propped his book on the steering wheel. I ran over, opened the passenger door, reached in, and shook his arm. He turned to me.

"Ma wants you," I said. "Right now. In the house."

Daddy took off his reading glasses, placed them to mark his page in the book, got out of the car, and headed inside.

Anne turned to me. "What's going on?"

Ma, Aunt Molly, and Daddy sat in the living room next to the radio, with Daddy sitting closest. And then we all heard it repeated: At 7:55 a.m., Hawaii time, Japanese planes had flown over Pearl Harbor and bombed the Pacific Fleet.

Ma and Aunt Molly looked at each other. "The boys," Ma said. "Thank God, they're not there." My uncles, all of whom had joined the army, were stationed on the East Coast. But they could all be sent overseas.

"We're in the war, for sure now," said Daddy.

***

President Roosevelt came on the radio the next day. We clustered around, listening. He talked about the Pearl Harbor bombing as "a day which will live in infamy." He then went before Congress to ask for a declaration of war on Japan. A few days later, Germany and Italy declared war on the United States.

Now, every morning, before Daddy left home to open the store and before I left for school, the radio came on and out came the big world map. Daddy unfolded it so that all of Europe could be seen. From that time on, he began to pencil the map with battle lines—German, French—and waited to see where British and American troops would be deployed. Perhaps because Daddy's relatives lived in Poland and Russia, he didn't pay as much attention to Japan. But I paid attention. I listened to every word.

I was already seeing the newsreels every Saturday afternoon. "The News of The Week" played before the start of the feature movie I saw each week. As the news spilled from Germany into our movie theater, I learned that Hitler had a plan. All disabled people were to be eliminated—gassed to death inside specially constructed trucks.[1]

I walked home from the movies with my friends—laughing and joking—to my sisters. Would they be eliminated, too, just because they were deaf?

I knew how to get scared. And every morning I looked at the maps again, watching. *How far away are they still?*

1. Some 200,000 to 350,000 disabled people are estimated to have been exterminated under the German Nazi regime during World War II.
"German Doctors and the Final Solution," Section 6, last modified September 21, 1986, https://www.nytimes.com/1986/09/21/magazine/german-doctors-and-the-final-solution.html?smid=em-share.

WORLD WAR II

While the storm clouds gather all across the sea
Let us swear allegiance to a land that's free
Let us all be grateful for a land so fair
As we raise our voices in a solemn prayer
God Bless America

At school we began to worry about reports that Japanese planes were seen approaching the California coastline. We spent hours figuring out how long it would take for the airplanes to reach us in Mount Vernon. Would we be able to get from home to school and back again? What would we do if we heard a plane overhead? Would we seek shelter in one of the apartment houses on Columbus Avenue or perhaps in a lobby? Though these buildings were surrounded by gates and open only to residents and their guests, surely a group of kids fleeing enemy warplanes wouldn't be turned away.

Which friends lived on our way home? Arlene? Carla? Perhaps we could seek shelter with them. No. *Not Carla.* . . . I would not, could not, seek shelter at Carla's house. I wasn't even sure that I wanted to walk to school with her again. Her family came from Germany, and, one day, on our walk to school, she'd told me her father hoped Hitler would win the war.

THE RED CROSS

On my way home from school, I often saw Mrs. Sherman walking straight and tall after her day at Red Cross headquarters. She wore a brown cap that matched her brown Red Cross uniform, with a patch over her left breast and epaulets on her jacket's shoulders.

I told my friend Margie about Mrs. Sherman.

"Maybe," said Margie, "just maybe we could go down to the Red Cross and volunteer. Remember how, at the movies, we see all those newsreels of volunteers—all those women from England in their uniforms?"

But, I thought, *the British are at war in a way that we aren't.* They were experiencing the bombings that we only feared.

When we went to the Red Cross offices in Mount Vernon, the receptionist smiled and said, "How nice of you girls to want to help. But there is nothing for you to do here. Perhaps your school can assist. Maybe they have projects."

As we headed back out the door, I said, "She acts as if we are imbeciles."

ROUTINES OF WAR

New routines developed. On the way to and from school, we looked along sidewalks and gutters for empty cigarette packs. Finding one, we pulled its wrapper apart, stripped out its tin foil, and added the foil to the foil ball we carried in our pocket. When a ball got big enough we'd turn it in at one of the special wartime recycling depots that took foil and other scarce wartime materials like rubber bands.

Knitting clubs were formed. Boys and girls met once a week to knit items for American soldiers overseas. Miles and miles of four-inch, khaki-colored, knit squares were turned into mufflers. The more accomplished knitters made mittens; knitters would slip encouraging notes into the finished pairs. And when the teacher wasn't looking, the more adventuresome added their names and addresses, hoping a grateful soldier would write back.

When the air raid siren sounded, teachers herded us into the hall where we were shown how to crouch and remain close to the floor, away from glass windows until a bell sounded, marking the end of the drill.

DADDY'S MAP OF EUROPE

The evening ritual continued. I watched as Daddy traced, again and again, his map marked with the location of the remaining members of his family—cousins, aunts, and uncles.

I watched as he traced the progress of the Allies. Together we read a news article that described how the Germans had locked one town's remaining Jews inside their synagogue and then burned the synagogue down.

Just as Mount Vernon was my hometown, Dubcha, in Russia, was Daddy's.

When Daddy was a young boy, his widowed mother had brought her five children to America to protect them from the Cossacks. The only stories Daddy told about Russia were about the Cossack raids. Every Easter he and his brothers hid in the rafters of their house to avoid being beaten and taken into the army, never to be seen again.

After leaving Russia, he knew nothing about his family who stayed there.

JUNIOR HIGH

I loved school. The sound of the bell. The lining up of boys at one door—the girls at the other. From the entrance into the large, wide corridor to the turn into one's homeroom, I found this never-ending sameness reassuring.

William Wilson Junior High was a place of certainty, whereas the world at war was not. In each class, I went to the seat I was assigned for the term. The teacher's desk always sat at the front. Students who most needed correcting sat at desks on either side of the teacher. When the bell sounded at the end of each class period, I knew where to go next.

The only surprises at school were waiting safely between the pages of books, chalked on a blackboard, or worked out on a piece of lined paper, with my name in the upper-left-hand corner, and the date underneath.

Spelling words were assigned on Mondays and tested on Thursdays. Tests were taken on long, narrow slips of paper, each word numbered in order. The teacher stood in front of the room clearly enunciating each word and using it in a sentence before repeating it.

Miss Murphy demanded excellence in science and rarely smiled. Mrs. Warner, my homeroom teacher, told us stories about her daughter; and while I knew there was no such thing as a school bell at home, I imagined how orderly the day must be at their house: each activity the same, with no surprises.

The tallest teacher at school, Miss Batcheldor, explained how pleased she was on the first day she'd come to teach at William Wilson because she'd been greeted by Miss Elmore, who was nearly as tall. We wove tales about those two. We said they were awaiting the return of fiancées overseas. But, after a time, we changed our story, endowing each with a lost lover, killed in action, or, at least, still among the missing. We could control the tragedies we created.

For me, school had always been a place of safety and friendship. In each school, as I progressed from grade to grade, I played in the band

and orchestra. And since starting junior high, carrying my clarinet to school also meant that even though I lived close enough to go home for lunch, I was allowed, because of music practice, to have lunch in the school cafeteria.

THE RARE SPECIMEN

Aline Flonase sat in the second row, two seats from the left of Mrs. Warner's desk. Each morning, the whole class watched Aline place her book bag on her desk and walk to the coat closet to remove and hang her coat, then return to her desk. We all wanted to see what she was wearing. Some mornings, she was dressed just like the rest of us: saddle shoes, thick white bobby socks, a plaid skirt, and a cardigan sweater buttoned down the back. Other mornings, she wore gauzy peasant blouses so transparent that her bra showed through.

On those days, we all knew what to expect. Mrs. Warner would stand and call Aline to her desk, place an arm around her shoulder, turn her away from our gaze, and whisper into her ear. On such days, Aline returned from lunch at home with a sweater thrown over her shoulders. She would slip on the sweater just as Mrs. Warner came back to the room.

Unlike Aline, the rest of us girls were only beginning to transition from undershirts with satin bows on the front to size A bras. We were always fearful that one of the boys would sneak up, place his fingers on our back, and snap the back of our bra strap. I don't know which was more embarrassing—to have your bra snapped or be still wearing an undershirt.

Aline was older, and the boys in our class steered clear of her. During recess, Aline told us about her Saturday afternoons at the rollerskating rink, where she met older boys. The boys were in high school or young men working while waiting to be drafted into the U.S. Armed Forces. We were impressed that Aline knew future soldiers, but I don't think we were envious. We regarded her as a rare specimen who'd drifted into our class. The important thing for us girls was to be like each other.

I especially wanted to fit in. I wanted to be seen like the other girls. I was tired of being introduced as "Her parents own The Fair on Fourth Avenue. . . . two deaf daughters. No. Not Miriam. She hears. But her sisters."

Other kids weren't introduced that way, were they?

A SCHOOL OF MY OWN

At home on weekends, Sylvia complained about her high school's job education program. "I hate using the sewing machines. So boring. And they teach us about housework. Not what I want . . . With the war on, lots of jobs for deaf girls. I want to go to work, like some of my friends."

"You are *not* getting a job packing lipsticks," Ma said. "There's no future in that. Back to school you're going! But not to Lexington."

"But enough of school. I want to get a job."

"So long as you live in this house, you go to school if I say so."

And that was that. Sylvia knew it.

Ma went to William Wilson Junior High School to inquire about enrolling Sylvia in the ninth grade. Sylvia and I weren't happy with Ma's decision.

"But it's my school," I cried. "I want it for me. Sylvia has the deaf school."

Even though most of my friends knew Sylvia, even though Sylvia joined us for our weekend stickball games—and gave us advice on everything—*this* was different.

I couldn't stop thinking about Aline and the stares she got. And Sylvia was even more different. What if the kids in Sylvia's class looked at her the way the kids in my class looked at Aline? What if they stared at me? What would I say if someone whispered about Sylvia? What would I do if she was teased?

Just as I had wanted to protect my relationship with my elementary school, I wanted to protect my place at my junior high.

"But why my school," I fretted to Ma. "It's my school. Sylvia's so much older. Everybody will ask, 'What's that big kid doing in ninth grade? Is she dumb or something?'"

"Sylvia always makes friends," said Ma. "Just you wait and see. She'll do fine. Every morning, you can walk to school together."

"Yeah," I said. "I know." When I wanted to talk with my friends, it would be some fun to walk to school with my eighteen-year-old sister. Ma didn't get it.

A HEARING WORLD

Now instead of going to her school for the week, Sylvia walked me to junior high.

"See," Ma said, "it's a hearing world and she fits right in. Look at the friends she's made, coming to the house to visit her."

And Sylvia did make friends. She even became the confidant, the older sister, to some of the kids at my school. Who could be safer to entrust your confessed crushes to than an eighteen-year-old deaf classmate? A boy named Dominick had a crush on her. He was sixteen and in her ninth-grade section. Instead of walking home from school with me, Sylvia and Dominick walked together.

Ma was pleased. "See what can happen . . . Going to school with hearing children . . . Sylvia will fit into the hearing world."

"But, Ma, he's younger than Sylvia. He's only sixteen!"

"Look, Miriam, it's the experience of being in a hearing environment. Making friends with hearing people. Having to rely on lipreading instead of signing with friends. Speaking to make yourself understood."

She continued. "I know that Sylvia will marry a deaf man. That's the way it should be. Deaf marry deaf." Ma listed all the couples she knew and pointed out the pitfalls when differences were great.

I asked Sylvia about Dominick. "Just a good friend," she said. "Not deaf. I'm not interested."

SYLVIA'S WARTIME JOB: RADIO ASSEMBLY TECHNICIAN

One morning as we walked to school, Sylvia told me about her plan to go to New York.

"But what will Ma say?" I asked.

"I'll tell her I'm meeting friends. I need to have some time with deaf people."

"And then?"

"Then I'm going to look for a job. Enough of this school with no deaf in it. Enough of being with little kids. All my friends are working. Wartime is a good time for deaf people to get jobs."

"But Ma doesn't want you packing lipsticks."

"I don't want to pack lipsticks. Other jobs. I'll look for other jobs." She nodded. "With friends who work in New York City."

The next day she pleaded with Ma and got permission to take a day off school to visit her deaf friends. Sylvia took the train to meet her friends who had jobs at radio assembly plants. She returned home that afternoon fully employed.

As a radio assembly technician she had a place to go each morning with other deaf people. She had found a good job without Ma paving the way, without anyone making phone calls to arrange an interview, without anyone trying to make the employer understand that deafness did not interfere with performance.

Ma was caught between her pride in Sylvia and her hopes that her oldest daughter would receive a more complete education. She consulted Daddy and afterward said "But I should have known. He always takes up for you kids."

The gentle advice Ma got from Sylvia's ninth-grade teacher was to the point. She'd had Sylvia in her class for two months. "She completed her schoolwork at Lexington, and she is older than the other students here. You can take pride in her independence. Perhaps, later, she can get more education—vocational training."

Back at my school, Sylvia's teacher spoke with me too. "I don't want you to feel as if Sylvia's leaving school has anything to do with you. We all understand," she said, "and we think no differently about you than we did before."

No differently than they did before? I was just a normal kid. Like everyone else.

WAR AT THE MATINEES

Even as the war was creating more factory jobs for deaf people, I continued to see war in new and shocking ways. It had become routine to see newsreels of the American war efforts at the movie theater. Otherwise, the public could only read about the war in newspapers or hear about it over the radio.

While my girlfriends and I cheered Allied victories and were saddened and frightened by news of defeats, war over in Europe had seemed far away. On Saturday afternoons at the movie theater, we saw footage of American soldiers getting ready for combat, of our soldiers fighting in Asia, and of the horrible destruction of our US Navy fleet in Hawaii.

We also began to notice small flags hung in windows. Not American flags, but American "service flags." The number of blue stars on a flag indicated the number of family members serving in the US Armed Forces. Over time, gold stars replaced blue stars. A gold star meant a son, brother, or husband had died in combat. It also meant that the mothers who looked out from those windows were called Gold Star Mothers.

"LEARN PRIVACY"

Ma turned away, back to her ironing. "You can't go. It's in New York City. You're too young."

"But Louie's just a friend. He lives right upstairs, Ma." There was no way I was going to change her mind. I knew this. But I tried. "Nothing bad will happen. You know that. And other girls in my class are invited."

"I don't care about the other girls in your class. It doesn't matter what anyone else is doing. You're not going to a fraternity party in New York City. And don't think your father's answer will be any different. Anyway, the store's busy, and he doesn't have time to listen to your complaints. If you want something to do, go help Daddy in the store."

***

I was in ninth grade. After school, the girls in my class were starting to wear lipstick, Tangee "Natural." We rubbed it on and rubbed it on, trying to get more color. It was so natural that it barely made your lips glisten. We wore shoes with heels. We carefully painted our legs with the orangey beige leg paint that was supposed to look like the silk stockings we couldn't get because of the war.

In September, we would attend A. B. Davis High School, we were sure that the boys in high school would be less silly—more sophisticated—than the boys in junior high. A date with Louie, my high school friend in the upstairs apartment, was my chance to move into that group early. But Ma had said, "No."

She was set on destroying my social life.

"My mother won't let me go," I complained, not wanting to explain to Louie that Ma thought I was too young.

Later, Louie's sister Diana told me that her brother had been warned, that their mother had foretold Ma's response. "I know Frances. There's not a chance she'll let Miriam go to a dance in New York City. Not even with you."

This was the first time I'd been asked on a date and it would have been so easy to go with a boy who was like an older brother, whose sister was one of my best friends, and whose family lived in the apartment right above ours. On the phone, I raged to my friends and discovered that just having been asked on a date impressed them.

When I told Sylvia, she nodded her head in sympathy. "Ma makes her own rules," she said. "Best thing to do is not say anything. Learn privacy. Works for me."

It was easy for Sylvia to have her privacy. All she had to do was sign to her friends. No one in our family knew what was said. And when she wanted a phone call made to a friend, she swore me to secrecy, and I made the call.

So it was no surprise to me when Sylvia announced she had a new boyfriend. I'd been calling Robert's mother for weeks to arrange times for Sylvia and Robert to get together. Sylvia's explanation for coming home late after work was to tell Ma she'd be having dinner with friends. If Ma objected, Sylvia pulled her usual line. "How many deaf people live here in Mount Vernon? No friends here." It always worked.

But there was no such line for me.

JUST LIKE THE PRINCESSES IN ENGLAND

There I was, finally, on my way to high school. Along with the rest of the world, I was learning about the Nazi extermination of the Jews and the extermination of people with disabilities.

Here I was, Jewish, dark-eyed, with curly auburn hair, and two deaf sisters.

In the midst of all of the war concerns, my parents announced we were moving.

"A corner lot and the builder will innovate to give us what we want," said Daddy.

"A lovely house with a center hall and fifty-seven windows," exclaimed Ma. "Miriam, you'll have a room of your own on the third floor, with dormer windows."

By myself . . . really? "Will I have an upstairs phone?" I asked.

"A phone? Why do you need a private phone? You can come downstairs when the phone call is for you. Is there anything so private you can't talk downstairs?" asked Ma.

Yes, I thought. *Yes. There are times when I don't want anyone listening.*

When the time came, I discovered that by pulling the phone cord to its full length and slipping into the hall closet with the boots and coats and gloves and hats, I could sit on the floor and no one could hear what I said.

Ma couldn't hear me. Shirley couldn't lipread my half of the conversation. Daddy had enough trouble understanding what was said even when I stood in front of him.

And so life went on. Just like the princesses in England. Even as bombs fell on London, we read how the princesses stayed with their parents in the palace. We continued knitting squares and mittens, conserving fuel, using ration coupons, and watching for stores that advertised shipments of silk stockings.

AIR RAID ALERT

When it was Daddy's turn to be our neighborhood air raid warden, he wore an armband and a helmet. He and the others wandered our streets with binoculars, identifying planes flying over Mount Vernon.

One evening when the alert sounded, Sylvia's latest boyfriend Robert was visiting. As Daddy headed out the door, he said, "Be sure to turn out the lights in the front room. I'll check outside to make sure the light from our kitchen isn't coming through our blackout curtains."

Ma wanted a light left on in the house so that Sylvia and Shirley could read lips if needed. She'd hung heavy black curtains beneath the draperies to blanket the house in darkness during air raid drills. Now, as she pulled the shades and drew the blackout curtains over them, she called me. "Tell Sylvia and Robert that there is an alert."

Standing in front of Sylvia and Robert, I spoke "Air raid alert. Lights out!"

Sylvia got up to help turn off the living room lights. But she kept the draperies open so we could watch the light disappear from the neighborhood as we awaited the "all clear" siren. Drivers pulled their cars to the side of the street and turned off their headlamps, and neighbors turned off table lamps and pulled down blackout curtains.

Robert turned the armchair to stare at the darkened street. Seeing only faint figures of men carrying flashlights dimmed with dark paper, I moved behind his chair. When I leaned forward, my hand brushed his shoulder. Robert reached up, clasped my hand in both of his, stroked it, and took it to his lips. Stunned, I pulled away. He'd kissed my hand, likely thinking I was Sylvia. I started to giggle. My shoulders shook as I laughed and laughed. Tears streamed down my cheeks.

When the "all clear" sounded, I quickly turned on the lights and grabbed Sylvia's arm.

"Sylvia, guess what happened?!" To demonstrate, I walked up behind Robert's chair, leaned over to peer through the window, and let my hand rest on his shoulder. This time, Sylvia's new boyfriend turned to look at me and my giggles started again. "When the lights were out," I said, "Robert kissed my hand! He thought I was you."

Sylvia grabbed my hand and signed to Robert. "Different? Can't tell my hand from Miriam's?"

Robert reddened. "Same to me. Feels the same."

I went to bed thinking, *What a great story to tell my friends!*

Part Four

Sylvia's Courtship

A MOUNT VERNON CHRISTMAS

Though storefront signs advertised free gifts and special discounts for soldiers in uniform home on leave, the magic of the Christmas holidays overtook Fourth Avenue, which transformed into a festival of lights. It was almost as if World War II had declared a time-out.

Merchants took pride in making Mount Vernon's six-block shopping district festive. Giant candles striped red and white like candy canes hung above the moving cars. Lampposts were wrapped in red streamers with strands of multicolored lights draped lamppost to lamppost.

Store windows displayed beautifully wrapped boxes with alluring merchandise nestled in layers of artificial snow. Mannequins posed in party dresses and furs next to mannequins dressed in shiny shoes and suits with red or green boutonnieres.

Santa Claus perched high on his throne in The Fair Store's large, second-floor window. Piles of gifts surrounded his chair. Santa's job was to give small presents and catalogs to the children who waited in line to sit on his lap and whisper a Christmas wish into his ear. Periodically, Santa looked out the big window and waved at the shoppers bustling along the avenue below.

By evening, once the long line of children had dwindled to none, Santa wearily climbed down from his throne. Walking to the steep staircase up to the third floor, he was careful not to disturb his costume. Once he was out of sight of the customers, he didn't worry about us as he stripped off his finery. Off came his hat, and with it, the matted white hair that encircled his brow. Reaching behind his ears, he unhooked the earpieces holding the snowy mustache and beard to his face. Suddenly he became an employee who'd otherwise gone missing.

Christmas really was my favorite time of year. Ma took over the small third-floor kitchen where she fixed meals in between helping shoppers. Carpet samples were rolled back on the second floor to make space for toys, games, sleds, and bikes. I wished for one thing after another, hoping what I selected as a Chanukah gift for myself wouldn't be sold to a customer.

***

When Shirley and I were very young, Sylvia explained this to us: "Don't tell your friends. But we don't believe in Santa Claus, because we're Jewish. But Christian children do. Their parents will be angry if you tell."

I knew that. It would be nice to believe in Santa. But I'd seen Santa without his beard.

SYLVIA'S COURTSHIP

Stationing myself on the sidewalk in front of Daddy's store, I offered, "May I help you?" as people walked past the display windows and toward the store doors.

I'd been hoping to catch a glimpse of my friends out Christmas shopping—or maybe on their way to the movies—but I was approached by a man with white hair and a heavyset woman. The man held his fedora in his hand and smiled at me as the woman threw her coat over her shoulder like a cape.

"Is Mr. Scharfman here?" she asked. "We're friends of his. We'd like to talk with him."

The woman's voice was familiar but I couldn't place it. Accompanying them to the entrance, I opened the door. Pointing toward Daddy's usual position at the cash register on the main floor, I said, "He's over there."

With an air of deliberation, the couple slowly walked into the store, intent on gazing about, as if to take it all in. And I followed. At Daddy's cash register, a salesperson tapped Daddy on the arm. "Mr. H.I., these people want to talk with you."

Daddy twisted the dial on his hearing aid as he turned to the couple. "How can I help you?"

"I am Gussie Bravin. And this is my husband, Morris. We are Carl's parents."

Now I knew why the woman's voice was familiar. I spoke on the phone with her at least twice a week when Sylvia asked me to call Carl. Tall, quiet Carl. It was Carl who met Sylvia after work in New York. It was Carl who escorted her to weekend parties. Sylvia and Carl had been dating for months. After Robert had left town to work on getting enough experience to obtain a union card, Sylvia and Carl had started seeing each other.

Sylvia brought Carl home to meet the family when she started going out with him. Ma had interrogated him. "Where did you go to school?

What trade did you study? Where are you working? How much money do you make?"

And Sylvia had fumed. "Why do you ask boys I bring home questions about their jobs? Always being nosy about my friends."

"I'm interested," said Ma. "I want to know what deaf people are being trained to do."

"I bet you never ask Miriam's boyfriends questions like that." Sylvia turned to me. "Does she?"

My friends were fourteen years old. "Nope," I said. "What can Ma ask? Do you march in the school band? Did you get good grades on your report card? Do you buy lunch at school or bring it from home?" I giggled so hard Sylvia couldn't lipread me.

Whenever Sylvia complained to Daddy about Ma, he said, "Your mother runs the house. She's in charge. I take care of the business." But on the occasion Ma had asked about Carl, he said, "Ma asks because we want to know. You are our daughter. It's important that you marry someone prepared to support a family."

"But that's my decision. You can't decide for me," said Sylvia. "You never question Miriam's friends."

"We know Miriam's friends," said Daddy. "It's different for deaf people. Harder to find a good job. Important to learn the right trade."

This brought Sylvia no satisfaction.

CARL'S PARENTS

Carl's parents had arrived unannounced during the store's busiest season. I raced upstairs to tell Sylvia. She worked the second-floor cash register, a temporary one set up in the toy department to avoid a downstairs holiday crush. Sylvia had been installed as a store cashier as soon as she'd turned sixteen. In our family, anyone old enough was expected to help. And, even now, with her factory job during the week, she was expected to help on weekends in Daddy's store.

Leaning over the sales counter, I tapped her shoulder. "Carl's parents . . . Carl's parents are coming up here with Ma and Daddy." It was hard for me to believe a boy's parents had come to the store to see Sylvia and meet our parents. I could hear Daddy's voice coming up the stairs. "Sylvia, Sylvia, they're almost here!"

Sylvia shrugged. "I knew they were coming. Carl told me they asked him many questions. They're here to see for themselves. You know hearing parents always nosy."

Just then, Mrs. Bravin saw Sylvia. "Why, that's Sylvia at the cash register," she exclaimed.

"How is Sylvia able to do that?" asked Mr. Bravin.

"Do what?" asked Daddy.

"Work. Take cash. Make change. Don't the customers ask questions?"

Ma cleared her throat. "And . . . why can't deaf people do jobs like that?"

I knew it! Ma was about to give her well-oiled lecture. How deaf people could do anything if they received the right training, were taught to lipread, and learned to live in the hearing world. Sylvia rolled her eyes as I lip-synced Ma's speech: *They can read the sales slip. They know how to count. Customers are happy to have their purchases quickly and efficiently taken care of.* According to Ma, working the cash register was a job suited for a deaf girl.

"Well . . . it's wonderful," said Mrs. Bravin. "And, of course, you're right."

THE FAIR PEOPLE

As it turned out, the Bravins had picked the right time for their unannounced visit. Daddy invited them to stay for the store's Christmas supper, and they sat with Ma, politely listening as Daddy thanked his employees with Christmas bonus checks.

***

Howie was the store manager and a solitary sort. Balding, with the start of a paunch, he was the store's only salesperson in the Basement Department. His life revolved around The Fair Store and the US Post Service. Early mornings he sorted mail, often carrying mail addressed to us at home to the store—just so our cards and letters weren't left waiting at home.

Eve was the store's tireless office secretary. She was devoted to Daddy and eventually taught each of us girls the magic of the adding machine.

Harry worked in the Window Shade Department surrounded by lengths of dowelling and bolts of precut linen for stapling into shades. When Ma wanted to go shopping, Harry picked her up and drove her to Fourth Avenue. When Ma needed a ride to the Lexington School for the Deaf, Harry drove her. Such car rides provided ample time for Harry to tell us his stories. Having attended his wedding, we knew all about his children. In fact, our family attended many employee celebrations. Our sales specialists were not only long-term employees; they were counted among our circle of friends.

***

Expressing appreciation for their year's work, Daddy forged ahead, seemingly oblivious to the murmuring that came from the tables the Fair Store employees had borrowed from our furniture department for the party.

The Fair people couldn't help it. As Carl arrived, they'd watched and whispered as he'd taken a seat at the end of Ma's table and engrossed himself in signed conversation with Sylvia. Their earlier introduction to Mr. and Mrs. Bravin meant Carl was not just another of Sylvia's boyfriends; after all, none of her other boyfriends' parents had appeared at the store.

"What's happening?" Sylvia asked every now and then, and I'd lip-sync Daddy: *Thank you. Thank you. Thank you.*

"Carl surprised to see his parents here?" I asked.

"No, he thought they might come. They wanted to meet Daddy and Ma. And because it's so busy during the holidays, they figured the best thing would be to stop by the store. But I am surprised Daddy asked his parents to stay for the store party.

"It's important that Carl's parents are here," I said. "The people want to know what's happening between you and Carl." Daddy's employees had known my sisters and me since we were little.

"Our business," said Sylvia. Turning her back to me, she signed to Carl and he firmly nodded in agreement.

THE RING

On Christmas morning Carl arrived at our house carrying a large, gift-wrapped box with a matching ribbon and bow. After saying hello to all of us, Carl nodded to the box.

"For Sylvia, " said Carl, and the two walked into the living room.

We knew what was going on, especially after Carl's parents had visited the store. I'd also overheard Ma and Daddy remark that Carl had a hearing brother. *Important.* No history of deaf people in Carl's family, even though we had a history in ours. And Carl would have a good job. He was being trained as a machinist, which meant a union job and steady employment.

When Sylvia walked back into the kitchen, she held out her left hand.

"Look! Look!" I shouted. "A ring!"

Sylvia grinned. Motioning to the jumble of boxes balanced in Carl's hands, she said, "Inside the big box was a smaller box. Then another . . . and another . . . then . . . finally a little box."

Daddy wrapped his arms around Sylvia and Carl and gave them a tight hug—both at the same time. "Mazel tov!" he said.

CHANUKAH CHRISTMAS

On December 25 when stores were closed and none of us was working, we celebrated Chanukah. Our Chanukah came late because Daddy and my uncles were all busy working during the weeks prior to Christmas. That was the busiest retail season. So on the most Christian of holidays, we celebrated Chanukah. But our celebration was still meaningful, especially to those of us who'd hinted for a holiday present. For the adults, even a late Chanukah was a joyful opportunity to socialize with family.

In a family like ours, presided over by a grandmother who got her due respect, holidays were celebrated in that grandmother's home. Grandma Bessie's cedar shake, two-story house with a wraparound porch was near a small retail area on Jamaica Avenue. The street was narrow and houses sat close together, separated by a narrow strip of yard divided in half by a hedge.

This was the house Grandma's children had purchased for her. After completing their schooling, they'd paid her back for her support. The younger boys, college graduates, now stationed at U.S. Army posts around the country, still called this house their home. It was where they returned on leave between the next assignments.

On Chanukah, no one was permitted to bring food to Grandma's house. Kosher ritual dictates a precise way to prepare food, and, observant of Jewish law, Grandma spent the preceding week preparing soups, vegetables, latkes, and strudel. Strudel dough—very thin dough for wrapping apples and nuts sprinkled with cinnamon and sugar—was stretched across the width of the enamel-topped kitchen table with Grandma watching for even the tiniest tear. When a tear emerged, she made a quick patch by carefully rolling over the dough.

"Ah," said Grandma, her hair caught back in a bun that slightly shook with each nod of her head. "Ah," she'd say again in satisfaction, as she cut the long roll into lengths that snugly fit onto the baking pan.

WHAT ABOUT ROBERT?

In 1942, December 25 belonged to Sylvia. When my nineteen-year-old sister walked into Grandma's kitchen with Carl, all the aunts and uncles packed into the kitchen with them.

"This is Carl," said Sylvia as she held out her left hand for all to see.

Grandma used Ma's Jewish name to ask, "*Fruma,* she's engaged? *Engaged?*"

"Getting married?" asked Aunt Ida.

"Sylvia getting married?" asked Cousin Marty.

"But I thought his name was Robert," said Aunt Blanche.

"What happened to Robert?" asked Uncle Mike.

"But weren't Sylvia and Robert going to get engaged?" asked Aunt Ida.

***

It was true. Sylvia and Robert had been planning to marry.

Carl was Robert's best friend. Robert had gone out of town to get needed work experience as a linotype operator. This experience would provide a union card, which then provided opportunities for a permanent, well-paying job with benefits at a New York newspaper. Robert, knowing that Sylvia was not the stay-at-home type and that, escorted or not, she'd attend social activities in his absence, called upon Carl to escort her to weekend parties until he got back.

It wasn't long before Sylvia told Ma and Daddy, "I'm in love with Carl."

Daddy said, "Last month you were in love with Robert."

Ma said, "You have a secure future with Robert. A linotypist is a very good job for a deaf person. Always employed. Secure."

"But I don't love Robert," Sylvia insisted. "I love Carl."

"How can you disappoint Robert while he is away from everyone he knows?" asked Ma. "What will you do?"

"Carl and I talked it over. We will wait until Robert gets his card and comes home. Then I will tell him," said Sylvia. "When he's home and finds out, he will have his friends. This way it won't stop him from getting his card."

***

"Robert went out of town to get his union papers," explained Ma. "Carl is Robert's best friend and offered to take care of Sylvia while he was gone."

"Some taking care of . . ." laughed Uncle Sam. "For life, he'll be taking care of her."

Grandma wiped her hands on her apron, carefully lifted the apron over her head, smoothed back her hair, and tightened the pins that held her bun in place. Looking at Sylvia, she gently pulled Sylvia's face close and kissed her. Grandma then turned to Carl—tall, quiet, and new to this family. She clasped his face and pulled him toward her. With this anointing, this blessing from Grandma Bessie, Carl was welcomed into our family.

WHAT IF . . . ?

"It's hard finding an apartment," said Sylvia. "Especially near friends. No car. We use the bus and subway. Near a subway, Carl and I can get to work."

Ma and Carl's mother had other concerns.

"What if they need help with something?" asked Mrs. Bravin.

"And in an emergency how will they get help?" asked Ma.

"No telephone."

"No one close by."

"Will the neighbors understand if they ask for help?"

"What if . . . ?"

The future mother-in-laws phoned back and forth, day after day, and the *what-ifs* continued.

***

Sylvia signed to Carl what their mothers had been discussing and he vigorously nodded. To Ma, Sylvia said, "We want to find our own apartment. We are getting married. Our decision."

Every weekend, Carl and Sylvia checked the newspaper classifieds for listings and set out to look at apartments. But it wasn't easy.

"Too dirty."

"Too far from deaf friends."

"Too long to travel to work."

"Too expensive."

In the meantime, Carl continued to live with his parents in their Bronx apartment and took the subway to Brooklyn. To become a machinist, he was attending night school. Once Carl completed his training and advanced in his job, the wedding date would be set.

"Carl will have a better chance for a good job with a good salary," Sylvia explained to me. "Better future as a machinist. We have to build for the future. Someday the war will be over. Hearing people will come back."

She sounded just like Ma. All those times Ma had asked Sylvia's boyfriends what their jobs were.

"Deaf people have to have good training to keep jobs," said Sylvia.

THE APARTMENT

One day, Carl's mother telephoned Ma. "There's an apartment for rent. I spoke to the super. If we give him a few dollars, Sylvia and Carl can have the apartment. It's one block from me."

"Call Sylvia," Ma told me. "Tell her to come down here."

I rushed to Sylvia's room. "Ma wants you," I said, shaking her shoulder so she'd pay attention. "Carl's mother is on the phone. Something about an apartment."

Sylvia watched Ma's lips. "Mrs. Bravin found an apartment. On Mount Hope Place. Right off the Grand Concourse. Close to the subway. One block from her apartment."

"How many rooms?" asked Sylvia.

Ma spoke to Mrs. Bravin. "She wants to know how large the apartment is." Ma listened, then turned to Sylvia. "Mrs. Bravin said you and Carl should come see it for yourselves. Daddy and I will drive you and we can all look at it together."

"No," said Sylvia. "It is our decision. Carl and I will look at it, and then you can see it if we decide."

"But we have to make a deposit to hold it."

"My life," said Sylvia. "We will see it first. Then it's your turn."

Ma shook her head, then spoke into the phone. "Sylvia will get there . . ." Turning to Sylvia, Ma raised her eyebrows and mouthed, *What time?* ". . . Sylvia says she will leave in a half-hour and meet Carl at your apartment, and then they'll go look at the apartment. My husband will drive her."

Ma hung up and said, "Daddy will drive you. He won't go in. You and Carl will go in, and if you like the apartment, call us, and we will come back and look at it too."

"Fine."

The apartment was on the third floor. It had one bedroom, a living room that Ma called nice-sized, and a kitchen. The bathroom was down the hall.

Sylvia grinned. "Privacy. Privacy for us."

Smiling, fingers flying, Sylvia and Carl talked to each other. Sylvia's signs were large and magnificent, encompassing the space beyond the boundaries of her body. Carl's were smaller, close to his chest, and contained. The way they signed represented their personalities.

As Sylvia prepared to move out of our family to form one of her own, I watched and learned. I, too, wanted independence.

THE BRIDAL DISTRICT

Sylvia stood erect in the center of the bridal shop as Ma held up dresses. The store proprietor, circling like a bird of prey, exclaimed approval at each dress held against Sylvia's shoulders.

Ma signaled me to hold the dress while she stepped back to consider. Positioned to see her reflection in the full-length mirror, she nodded at each of Ma's selections. How different this sister seemed from the sister I knew; she was letting Ma make all the decisions.

From bridal shop to bridal shop, this scene repeated itself. Fortunately, the shops were concentrated within blocks of each other. The narrow, first-floor bridal shops in New York's Garment District rested below tenement apartments. Fire escapes dominated building fronts, and the city's canyon-like streets blocked the light from shop windows.

Sylvia's dress was just one item on the wedding checklist. Many more trips to New York's Lower East Side followed. Dresses had to be selected for the bridesmaids, who were Sylvia's school friends she'd known for all of her life.

One evening, Sylvia turned to me and said, "Miriam, will you be in my wedding?"

I was ecstatic. "In your wedding? With all your deaf friends?" Those girls were like big sisters to me.

"You will be my maid of honor," said Sylvia. "But your dress is up to me. You have to wear what I pick. The dress has to look good on all the bridesmaids."

Sylvia met her friends after work and they scoured the shops on New York's Lower East Side. Then it was my turn to stand on the small stool, staying still while modeling the dress Sylvia and her friends had selected. It had a full skirt, sweetheart neckline, and gauzy overskirt. It was too big.

At fourteen, taller than Ma, shorter than Sylvia, I weighed ninety pounds.

"But what if it doesn't fit?" I asked.

"We ordered them in the correct sizes," said the saleslady.

Holding the bodice against me, turning, and turning again, I bunched the extra fabric in my hands to see how it would look when the dress was the correct size.

"Believe me. It will fit perfectly," said the saleslady. "Perfectly."

SYLVIA'S WEDDING DAY

If Ma could get Sylvia dressed for her wedding, the months of preparation would be over. And if all went according to plan, I'd have a room of my own.

Sylvia was just three hours from becoming a June bride. To keep the train of Sylvia's wedding dress unwrinkled, Daddy balanced the dress's hanger on the molding around the dining room ceiling.

All the neighborhood kids were playing ball in the street. I'd just run inside to change my clothes for the wedding. Ma tapped Daddy on the arm. "Come here."

Daddy looked out the window. "Did you ever see anything like that?" asked Ma. Sylvia was at bat, waiting for a pitch. "Just look at her!" complained Ma. "She's playing stick ball with the kids in the neighborhood when she's about to get married."

"Miriam," she turned and said, "go back out there and tell her to come inside. She had her nails done yesterday and I don't want them broken. It's time for her to bathe and get ready. . . . And, Miriam, take your clarinet to the wedding. You can play something for the guests."

My face got hot at her suggestion. "No! This is Sylvia's day. Not mine. This is a wedding, not a recital. . . ."

"Take it," Ma repeated.

Instantly I decided I would conveniently forget the clarinet and leave it at home. I knew Ma would be too busy to remember. But, just in case, I slipped the clarinet under my bed. I could always say I'd left it in the band room at school.

***

The wedding location was not far from where Carl's parents lived in the Bronx, and somehow we managed to get Sylvia there on time.

The wedding caterer, who was doubling as the wedding planner, directed Shirley to sit with our cousins and cued the bridesmaids, ushers, Carl, and Mr. and Mrs. Bravin to take their places. As Sylvia's maid of honor, I preceded the bride down the aisle. She then approached with

Ma and Daddy walking on either side of her. At the chuppah, Ma and Daddy took their place with the Bravins.

The ceremony began. Sylvia and Carl faced the rabbi. With no sign language and no familiar face to lipread, the couple struggled to follow what the rabbi said. But because they had practiced voicing their parts to each other in Hebrew, their vows came easily. By the end, the newlyweds walked back up the aisle smiling and waving and disappeared.

The rest of us filed into the dining room, found our tables, and awaited the couple. When the band leader said, "Let us give a warm welcome to Mr. and Mrs. Carl Bravin," the caterer cued them to enter. The band struck the notes for the first dance and Sylvia and Carl joined together. Sensing the music through the floor's vibrations, they danced across the room. Ma and Daddy joined in, as did Carl's parents. Then everyone began to dance and change partners. My uncles, all wearing army uniforms, gathered my female cousins and me and led us onto the dance floor. Cousin Marty, soon to be inducted and sent overseas, grabbed whichever cousin was closest, jitterbugging with each of us until we begged him to stop.

Ma had spent months considering the menu, but we hardly noticed the food. The newlyweds cut their wedding cake and fed each other. It wasn't long before they'd changed into their traveling clothes and climbed into a cab. Kisses went around. And then my big sister was gone.

Part Five

Where Do Your Sisters Go?

PUH-TA-TOES AND *PUH-PEES*

Shirley was chauffeured to and from the Lexington School by Ma and her driver, Harry, from The Fair Store's Window Shade Department. On this day, I went with them. As we neared the school's dreary Victorian entrance, I noticed how Shirley's tight corkscrew ringlets shone in the morning sun. Ahead of us, a long line of young girls stretched through the shadowy doorway to the cramped waiting room inside. There, each child signed in, with a parent waiting to make sure staff knew the child was now under school supervision.

As classes commenced, one student—sometimes a group—was called into the office of the school speech pathologist, Miss New. It was there that a familiar lesson began. Looking into the face of Miss New, the child was to repeat the sound needed to enunciate a word. When a child had difficulty saying, for instance, the soft sound for the letter *P*, Miss New said, "Puh." *Puh*, she'd say, as she held the paper in the palm of her hand close to her lips. *Puh* and the paper flew out of her hand and landed on the floor. Miss New's feet were surrounded by tiny pieces of tissue paper she'd torn from the larger sheet she held in her hand.

"Puh," she'd say, as she held another scrap close to the student's lips. "Puh-ta-toe," she'd say, before holding the next scrap close to the student's lips. On the table were visual cues—perhaps a real potato or a picture of a puppy. "Puh-pee." When it came Shirley's turn, it was Shirley who floated the snowy pieces of tissue paper to the floor. Ma's lips moved silently—*Put*—as Shirley struggled with the sound of a particular teacher's name. *Puh.*

Rules were the same as at my school. You stood when a teacher entered the room. You raised your hand when you wished to speak. But, here, it wasn't quite enough to say, "Good morning, Miss Bennett." Miss Bennett's ear would be tuned to the sound of your speech.

MA'S HATS

Later that year, Ma met her friend, Mrs. Tracy, for lunch at Schrafft's.

Mrs. Tracy was the wife of actor Spencer Tracy and the founder and director of the John Tracy Clinic, named for their deaf son. Mrs. Tracy had come to visit East Coast programs for deaf children.

During lunch, Mrs. Tracy shared a conversation she'd had with her priest. She'd asked why she, a devout church member, had a deaf son. But, for decades into my future, I'd find it consistent with what I would hear as I counseled parents who had kids with various types of issues and who struggled in bewilderment to get things right. So, what could religion offer Mrs. Tracy in terms of understanding? The priest explained: God only chooses special people who possess the ability to parent a special child.

Ma had responded with skepticism, telling Mrs. Tracy that she (Ma) must be very special, then, because she had *two* deaf children.

***

Ma's increasing knowledge of deaf education, teacher training, and supports for families raising a deaf child (or deaf children) often took her into New York City. She gathered a group of mothers to work with her in setting up the first parents' group for the Lexington School for the Deaf. Today, we would call this a support group. In Ma's time, there were few models. It wasn't until the 1970–80s that the concept was popularized and then run primarily through groups initiated by educational institutions, hospitals, and other agencies working with families (and individuals) with similar concerns and needs.

Ma was ahead of the curve.

The women bonded over the support of their kids and, along the way, became activists. The mothers always had questions—and suggestions. The most important were taken to Dr. O'Connor, the Lexington superintendent.

The pleasure Ma got from these friendships was evident. She came home with stories and questions raised. Once in a while, she returned from "The City," as she called it, with a hat box containing a new hat—one looking much like a flight of fancy. Her face beamed as she anticipated our reactions.

***

Ma's favorite hat shop, where hats were fashioned to the customer's wishes, was on Madison Avenue in the City. Ma was a valued customer. Some years she often walked in to inquire about a new chapeau. Purchase of a new hat was a signal that Ma had worries from which she sought diversion. And a new hat was always the solution.

Picking up one sample and then another, she'd place a hat on her head. Closely eyeing herself in the mirror, she'd turn her head to one side and then to the other while smiling her artificial, hat-trying-on smile. Taking off the hat, she'd take the comb from her purse and run it through her short, gray hair. Then reaching for the next, she'd begin again—approving and disapproving in turns—commenting on its shape, depth of crown, curve of brim.

Meanwhile, the milliner attentively listened, occasionally going to the back room to bring out more samples. Once Ma decided on the shape of the hat, she and the milliner decided on its decorations. They hovered over boxes of beads, feathers, ribbons, and fancy pins. As Ma picked out one ornament after another, the milliner held it in place, then moved it around. Flowers, birds, and buckles were perched to nestle against the crown. Feathers were arranged to either tuck around the base of the crown or graze the edge of the brim.

Decisions made, deposit paid, a date agreed for the hat to be ready, Ma put her soon-to-be-replaced old hat back on her head and went out the door.

WHERE DO YOUR SISTERS GO?

The most flamboyant of Ma's hats was shaped like an improbable bird perched to take flight. Made of gold felt with a band around its crown, the hat was adorned by two gold feathered wings. Ma wore it home from her next lunch in the city.

"You have got to come to the parents' meeting," she said. "You have to talk to those women."

"About what?" I asked.

"About your relationship with your sisters . . ."

***

Ma was giving Shirley a birthday party at school and I'd gone to help. But Ma's real need resurfaced when she mentioned the school's parents group meeting.

"This will be a perfect opportunity," said Ma. "You will be our guest speaker."

"But, Ma, I don't want to do it. What am I going to say?!"

"Miriam, you don't know the problems these mothers have. They need you. They need to hear about how you and Shirley and Sylvia get along."

"You mean they need to know how I have to take Shirley with me to the movies all the time? They need to know that sometimes she's a pesky little sister? . . . Those kinds of things? How Sylvia and her friends tease me when they visited on weekends? Is that what you want me to tell them?"

"Yes," said Ma. "Whatever you want."

***

The mothers had seated themselves in a circle. Ma's friend Jan, who kept the group's minutes, introduced me.

"Frances' daughter," Jan was saying, "Most of you know Shirley and Sylvia. Well, here's Miriam, the middle daughter. She'll tell us what it's like to live with two deaf sisters."

Silence. What did they want from me? I was fifteen. My eyes traveled the ceiling. Like all the classrooms at Lexington, the ceiling was as high as the room was wide. I belonged somewhere else.

More silence. How to begin?

"Well . . . I live at home with Shirley. Sylvia's married, you know. She works in New York. . . . I do my homework in the breakfast room at home. Shirley is only seven and doesn't have homework. But my mother keeps her busy working on language and speech. Shirley does her work in the breakfast room with me."

One mother raised her hand. It felt weird for a parent to raise her hand to get my permission to speak. I nodded and she asked, "What do you do when your friends come to your house?"

"Well . . . maybe we go to my room and talk. Maybe we go downtown to Fourth Avenue. Maybe we go skating. It depends on what we want to do."

"No, no," said the woman, "that's not what I mean. What do you do if your sister is home?"

"Well, Shirley is always home. And, on weekends, Sylvia and her husband come home for a visit . . . or, I have to drag Shirley with me to the movies."

"But what do you do if your friends come over and your sisters are there? Where do they go?"

"Where does *who* go?"

"Where do your sisters go?"

"I don't understand."

The mother paused and tried to explain. "My other children . . . When their friends come over . . . They don't want their deaf sister around. They say they're embarrassed. They say their friends don't understand what she says."

The mothers looked at me. Their heads nodded in agreement. What was I to say but the truth?

"My sisters know my friends, and I know their friends." "But what if . . . What if your friends don't understand what your sisters are saying?"

"I interpret. Or Sylvia and Shirley repeat." I grinned. "I always know when my friends don't understand . . . They get stupid smiles on their faces—like they're pretending to understand. When that happens, my friends look so dumb." I laughed out loud. "When that happens, I step in and tell them what my sister said."

I watched as the women turned to each other, some nodding, others just shaking their heads.

And I wondered, weren't they all part of the same family?

BIRTHDAY PARTY

Later that morning, as Ma and I carried birthday cake and candles into Shirley's classroom, I told Ma, "I never want to do that again. I don't know what to say to those mothers."

Hidden away when friends came to visit? What that mother had said would stick with me.

***

Eight little girls sat with their teacher at a round table. Being able to see faces was essential to learning and verbal communication for deaf students.

Sign language was forbidden and could mean a visit to the principal's office. The Lexington School agreed with the oralism movement, where the focus was on "aural habilitation." Sign language, it was believed, impeded the acquisition of aural skills. This was a topic continually addressed in our home.

While Ma agreed that my sisters could sign to each other, she insisted they use their voices to communicate with the rest of us. In keeping with this principle of aural communication, neither Ma nor Daddy used sign, nor did I—at least not in the presence of my parents. Sylvia, Shirley, and I managed to understand each other through lipreading and gesturing—and when out of the sight of our mother—through my limited ability to sign.

***

As Ma and I entered Shirley's classroom, the little girls pointed to us and then turned to face each other to voice their excitement. When their teacher, Miss Bennett, switched the overhead light off and on they instantly turned their faces toward her.

Careful to enunciate and speak slowly, Miss Bennett asked, "What's special about today?" The girls responded without hesitation. "Shirley's birthday!"

Shirley's party was like any other birthday party in any other elementary school, with the exception that each child was instructed to focus on the lips of classmates as they sang the birthday song and, in turn, they were to answer the same question: "How many candles on the cake?" But, first, came their teacher's lesson.

Miss Bennett pointed to each word in a list of words written on the blackboard. As she pointed to each word, she held up its matching item, and the girls repeated together:

party
birthday
candles
birthday cake
hats
baskets
ice cream

Once the words were spoken, the birthday party began with Shirley standing at the front of the room. The students raised their voices in unison. "Happy Birthday!" Shirley watched their lips as they sang to her, and they watched Shirley as she blew out the candles.

"How wonderful," said the teacher. "How wonderful."

Turning to Ma before turning to me, Miss Bennett smiled. "Why, you're the only child in your family that I haven't had the opportunity to teach in my class."

When the teacher turned back to her students, I told Ma I was going out into the hall.

THE TOO FAMILIAR

The long corridors of the Lexington School for the Deaf on 67th Street and Lexington Avenue in New York City were as familiar to me as the hallways of my own high school in Mount Vernon. The school's upper-floor corridor led to parents' meetings. All the other heavy oak doors led to vocational training for the school's older students, who'd completed eighth grade like Sylvia. Shirley's classroom was on the ground floor with the rest.

***

Lexington School was where Shirley and the other little girls in her class learned to work and play together. Enrolled in the school's nursery program at ages three through five, they were initially corralled in rows of playpens. Eventually, they went outside to the school's playground. Protected by a tall iron fence, they'd climb the jungle gym and swish through the air on swings.

I knew these girls. They were toddlers when I first met them. Even now they were just little kids. *Hidden away when friends came to visit?*

***

Out in the corridor, I heard a voice leak through a heavy oak door every now and then. A teacher's instruction, a child mimicking a sentence, a word, a sound. A few steps farther and I stood outside the auditorium with its open doors. Girls were learning words to songs as they stood around a piano. With their hands flattened to the piano top, they absorbed the rhythmic vibrations as the piano's hammers hit its strings. I kept walking until two students farther down the corridor turned toward each other. Pausing, I watched as they pulled their hands close to their bodies, so as not to be noticed, and signed to each other in small, furtive, hand movements. Students who pledged not to sign were awarded school medals. But if caught signing, medals were taken away.

So how had many of the Lexington students learned sign language? I had learned sign language through Sylvia, of course. Sylvia had learned to sign in the dorms at night from the students with deaf parents—at least, parents who signed—and by dorm counselors who were deaf.

***

At home, with Shirley asleep, I stretched out on the leatherette seat in the breakfast room to finish my homework with the radio playing. I could hear Ma talking to Daddy.

"There we were," said Ma, "the birthday cake waiting to be cut . . . And what do you think the teacher said?"

"What?" asked Daddy.

"Miss Bennett turns to Miriam and says, 'Why, you're the only child in your family whom I've not had the opportunity to teach.'"

"So?"

"So, what does she need? Another deaf child? Two aren't enough from one family?"

ALWAYS THE SAME

A strange car would park in front of our house and I'd know. Even before I'd walked to the back of the house and come in through the kitchen door, I'd know. Another baby. Another family who'd heard about my sisters and my parents.

It was always the same. Ma would say, "This is Miriam," and the couple would look in my direction. I'd say, "Hi," and the father or the mother would say, with some surprise, "Oh. You hear . . . You're the hearing daughter."

I'd wander away, back into the kitchen, leaving Ma to talk with her visitors. If the baby was really cute, I'd offer to take the baby with me. From the kitchen, I could hear what was said. It was always the same conversation. Ma explained how both Sylvia and Shirley were deaf from birth. Next, she'd elaborate on the importance of a good education. "My girls get speech lessons. They know how to lipread. I expect the same from them as I do from Miriam. No free rides just because you're deaf."

I could imagine the parents' eyes widening because I'd seen it so many times. Then Ma would make it a point to add, "It's a hearing world."

No matter how carefully the parents tried couching the next question, it always came out the same. "We don't know why our baby was born deaf. The doctors have no answer—and there's no deafness in our families . . ."

Then looking at Ma, one of them would ask, "*And, in your case?*"

And Ma would say, "We have no answers either."

HEARING AIDS FOR DEAF KIDS

The hearing aids of the 1940s amplified sound. Daddy, at least, could hear. Though not all of the time. Not in noisy environments. Not from a distance.

Sylvia and Shirley could not hear and yet were reluctant to wear hearing aids. None of Sylvia's deaf friends wore them. Hearing aids held no charm, after all—they were irritating, bulky, and oftentimes too visible. And for the many who were profoundly deaf, hearing aids provided little or no improvement. But no matter. Every child at the Lexington School was expected to use one, whether it helped or not.

Yet I don't remember Sylvia ever wearing one. Shirley, who had more residual hearing than Sylvia, began to wear an aid at school and occasionally at home. By age twelve, Shirley simply refused because they bothered her.

She said that everyone knew she was deaf, and to get her attention they could just touch her shoulder. When she wore aids, people forgot she was deaf, didn't face her, talked faster, assumed she could perfectly hear.

She threw her aids away into a public trash can.

Part Six

Me in My Own World

GROWING PAINS

While I felt certain my sisters would go on to have full lives, I began to feel that my own life as "Miriam Hearing Sister" might be where my life would end.

I'm not sure when I began feeling this way. Had it started with Sylvia's wedding and her move to an apartment? I didn't think so. Had it started when I spoke to the parents' group? Or later that day when I'd walked the school's corridors, suddenly realizing that I knew those corridors as well as I knew the hallways of my own school? Was it because I knew every classroom and almost every teacher, that all the teachers knew me; and that I'd heard about every school assembly, every student award, every school rule, and every parent complaint at my sisters' school? Or was it afterward when Ma said to Daddy: "Aren't two deaf children in our family enough?"

Always introduced as "the girl with two deaf sisters," I wanted to be *the girl with auburn hair and freckles. The girl who lives in the house on California Road. The girl who plays clarinet. The girl who marches in the school band. The girl who loves to dance. The girl who reads the most books.*

I wanted to be me.

ME IN MY OWN WORLD

Packed away in a little-used drawer was an old family photo album. One picture shows me on a family outing at a state park. There is a picnic table, a fire in a stone barbecue, and a playing field circled by picnickers. And there I am skinny, curly-haired, dressed in a striped polo shirt and too-large shorts. Wearing glasses and lying on a blanket, I am curled around a book. I look like a giant comma.

Hoping to read my way through the full alphabet of authors, I'd begun at the local library with last names beginning with A. By the time of this photograph, I'd read through the Children's Section and was well into the Young Adult Section. Through reading, I'd found a space for myself.

As my sisters dwelled in their world of deaf friends and sign language and special schools, I began to build a parallel universe that was my own. Separate.

When Sylvia brought friends home from school and their teasing became too much, I collected my books and went to a different space in the apartment to cut off their voices and signs. Other times, Ma had complained that, when reading, I either didn't hear or I answered, "In a minute," which might stretch into hours (if I was lucky).

Years later, when I was in college, Daddy asked that I share my list of required readings. He went to the library and read along with me. At age sixty-one, he finally started college himself, attending evening classes at New York University.

RELIGIOUS EDUCATION

Perhaps my devotion to books was what led me to rebel against religious training.

Weekly classes at the local Conservative synagogue often repeated lessons from the week before. Such an approach allowed students with infrequent attendance to catch up, but slowed me, squelching my desire to learn more. Finally, when the Hebrew letters started to be retaught each week, I refused to attend classes.

Daddy supported me in this. When the rabbi asked when I would return, Daddy said, "When real learning takes place. My daughter wants to learn."

***

For me, the observance of Jewish holidays was less about prayer and ritual than about family and friends. By walking from one synagogue to the next, I got to spend time with friends equally eager to escape long services, and it gave us girls a chance to compare outfits. One year I wore a pair of bright red pumps—a bit of magic that caused me to stand straighter and taller and that drew envious glances.

Traversing much of Mount Vernon, my friends and I visited the two Reform temples and the two Conservative synagogues. We did not go to the Eighth Avenue synagogue because it was out of the way and more importantly, Orthodox. Our Orthodox classmates wouldn't lounge outside on the synagogue steps; they'd be inside with their parents for the long morning service.

***

Sometimes our family traveled to Spring Valley, New York, where uncles and aunts congregated for Passover at Aunt Ida's house. The Seder meal was prepared in concert with the uncles saying prayers. Then we walked to the *shul.*

The small synagogue near Aunt Ida's house sat at the edge of a pasture frequented by slow-moving cattle. Unaware of this incongruity, neither was I overcome with emotion at the emerging surround of early daffodils.

In family photographs, two plaid suits are shown: one in muted tones of blue, beige, and brown; the other in red tartan. First worn by Sylvia, for whom they were purchased, then handed down, first to me and then to Cousin Dorothy, and finally to Shirley. Year after year, family photographs show us garbed in one plaid or the other.

Our spring plaids notwithstanding, my sisters and I sat restively with Ma and Daddy. The murmurs of congregants cushioned the sound of the rabbi's prayer as he chanted and bowed with his back to the congregation. Daddy turned the pages of the *siddur*, pointing to the location of the words to the service.

Pointing to her purse, Sylvia winked at me and nudged Shirley before pulling out three small books. Novels!

Each fit nicely into a prayer book. Sylvia demonstrated that by bending our bodies forward we could keep anyone sitting behind us from looking over our shoulders and seeing a page of English where a page of Hebrew should be.

She slipped each of us a novel, then signed to me, "Tell us when we have to stand." As the hearing sister, it was my duty to stay in sync with the service. No matter how mesmerizing the chapter, it was my duty. If we continued to sit when everyone stood, we would look ridiculous, and our secret would be discovered.

ADRIFT AMONG JEWS

Perhaps my adolescent rebellion had been defined for me.

With no malachan angels watching over me, I found no solace in prayer. I didn't believe in a deity who stood at my shoulder to monitor each morsel eaten or each act committed.

Theologically I was adrift. Ma was an observant Jew and Daddy abided by her precepts (though he worked on Saturdays at his store), and we typically attended synagogue only on Jewish holidays or during annual religious services in memory of a departed relative.

Untethering myself, I was about to move out of the synagogue and into the sphere of social-political engagement—a place where a protest was not only acceptable but desired. Unlike Sylvia, I wouldn't be coming home late with a grin on my face and a sparkle of mischief in my eye as I imitated lobster pincers behind Ma's back—a sure sign to me that Sylvia had eaten seafood for dinner.

My passage toward independence would be activism. But I wouldn't be moving far from my Jewish roots.

***

I met Mrs. Freedman when I joined a Zionist youth movement. Young Judea met in Mrs. Freedman's living room week after week.

"Girls," she'd say, "stand up straight. Raise your voices to the coming of the new Jewish State." With that, we stood in our plaid skirts and cardigan sweaters buttoned down the back, with our brown and white saddle shoes firmly planted to the floor. Sometimes we sang off-key, but with a fervor lit by Mrs. Freedman.

Initially, the appeal of the group was the opportunity to gather after school in an activity that had parental approval without parent involvement. Looking back, I see how the Young Judea group, with its emphasis on Jewish identity and social action, enveloped the ideals of our families. More importantly, we were under the guidance of a woman well-known in the community.

Pamphlets and articles were strewn around Mrs. Freedman's living room. On a bulletin board in the hallway leading into her kitchen were other articles; they were hard to miss if you walked down that hall. Especially when she called after you, "Look at the article from the *Times* (or from the *New York Post*, or the *Herald Tribune*)."

Mrs. Freedman had a way of personalizing each international conflagration. Eyeglasses sometimes sliding down the bridge of her nose, she educated us on the impact on ordinary people. I began reading newspapers with an eye toward learning about other places and people who had their own obstacles to overcome.

Mrs. Freedman lit my pathway to an understanding of the Jewish people and our history—transporting me beyond the immediate concerns of my family. She gave me a chance to try out ideas and voice my frustrations. She listened, counseled, and was ever-present when I needed to talk. Mrs. Freedman became the catalyst for broadening my understanding of alternative expressions of Judaism and presented choices and a path where I could define myself.

THE SUMMER OF 1945

Summer began with a news story of a death in a deaf family. A baby died. Perhaps a blanket smothered the baby. A crib death. Little was understood.

Word spread through the deaf community to hearing parents of deaf married children.

"How will they know if the baby cries or needs help?" asked Mrs. Bravin.

"Sylvia and Carl will have to move into our house," said Ma.

That was the only solution—no matter that infant suffocation wasn't unique to deaf parents, and no matter how many deaf couples had succeeded in raising their children for decades, even centuries.

***

My bedroom was the room away from all the other rooms in our house. I could only reach it by climbing the stairs to a large third-floor landing. Through the door to the right, I entered my small personal space.

That summer, I moved from my room on the third floor, the room where my bed nested against the side wall, the room with the sloping ceiling and two small windows where I could look out into the treetops and onto the flowering gardens that belonged to the estate across the road.

Carrying my belongings down the stairs, I took with me the memories of a room and a view of the world that had been all my own.

THE BABY BUZZER

On weekends, Sylvia and Carl came to plan their new home on the third floor of Ma's and Daddy's house. An accumulation of boxes and discarded furniture was cleared, and the landing was enclosed with a wall and door. The landing became a small kitchen and living room. Slowly my tiny nest became their three-room apartment with a bathroom.

"Not like our apartment in the Bronx," said Sylvia, "but safe for the baby."

***

Ma moved me into her favorite room of the house on the second floor amid the other bedrooms.

"See," she said, "here you'll have *two rooms*. The small room off the sitting room for your desk. Fill the drawers—all yours. And here . . . your bedroom with windows all around and two beds. You'll be able to invite a friend to a sleepover. This is better than upstairs. You'll love it."

Eventually, I made my peace with the new room. As I began filling the cubby holes of the desk and arranging my books, I discovered that the door to the sitting room could be closed, and I regained a sense of privacy.

***

Sylvia and Carl would share their new third-floor bedroom with their baby.

But for safety's sake, Carl installed a buzzer on the staircase banister to ensure that Ma and I could easily buzz their apartment whenever we heard their baby cry. The buzzer was more like a doorbell that didn't ring. When pressed, it caused the lamp in their bedroom to flicker on and off to alert them to the baby's crying. Carl had wired the so-called buzzer to the electrical outlets.

Carl's aptitude for modification eventually led him to create a device that vibrated when it detected sound waves such as a ringing doorbell or a crying baby. Deaf members of the community could tuck a disk under their pillow and be awakened during the night.

***

I had taken a summer job waitressing at a summer camp in Maine. I hadn't yet left before the family surprised me by setting up the baby's bassinet and crib in my second-floor sitting room—sure signs that Sylvia and Carl didn't expect to spend all their time upstairs in their new third-floor suite.

CAMP HOMESICK

My first experience away from my family came with an aching for home.

Separating the pain in the pit of my stomach from the demands of my summer job was hard to do. If any symptom showed, all my feelings might pour out. So, each morning I practiced smiling into the mirror as I steeled myself against homesickness. Gradually, I realized how to get by: get lost in a book, spend time with others, and do what I'd come to do: wait tables.

Three times each day the camp's wait staff set tables and served food to more than 100 campers and, after each meal, cleaned the mess hall. The work was hard, not as fun as the camp directors had led us to believe. At sixteen, fun came from free run of the camp when we weren't working and from hitchhiking into town on our day off.

I shared my room above the mess hall with three other girls. We were down the corridor from the camp director's suite and across the hall from the head counselor's infant. Quiet hours started early so that the counselor's baby could sleep.

Knowing that when camp ended, I'd go home to a houseful of family and a new baby pulled me through that summer.

BEAUTIFUL BABY BOY

I will always connect Philip's birth with the Japanese surrender.

The end of World War II was announced over camp loudspeakers on August 15, 1945.

Eleven days later, news of my nephew's birth came by way of a phone call from Ma. "It's a boy," she said. "Named Philip. Healthy. Adorable. He'll come home from the hospital next week when you're home from camp."

In my mind, our family's abundant joy for the first birth in our family's next generation equaled a global celebration.

***

Home from camp that following week, I ran into the house shouting. "I'm home!" No response. I ran up the stairs to the second-floor landing, my duffel bag dragging behind me. Ma started down from the third floor.

"Where is everyone?" I asked. "When do I get to see the baby?" Then, noticing Ma's red, swollen eyes, I asked, "What's wrong?"

"Nothing," she assured me. "Nothing. Just a sty on my eyelid."

***

At the hospital, Sylvia told me all about the baby's birth. How she'd been wheeled down the corridor afterward. How she'd called to the elder Bravins and Ma and Daddy, how she signed to Carl. "It's a boy! It's a boy!"

The firstborn of our next generation was a boy. Sylvia and Carl had a son.

"And you will be godmother," Sylvia said to me. "Godfather will be Uncle Eddie."

***

I held my tiny nephew, hugged him close, peered into his beautiful baby face, and together we brought him home.

***

As the baby lay on the bassinet in the sitting room, I heard Ma whistle. It was a haunting, one-tone, high-pitched whistle, just as I'd heard when Shirley was a baby. These were the only times I ever remember Ma whistling.

Between homework and dates with boys, talking on the phone, and practicing my clarinet, I played with my red-haired godchild—*my beautiful, deaf, nephew, baby Philip.*

Part Seven

Life or Death Choices

DECISION TIME

At regular intervals during my senior year at A. B. Davis High School, a list of student names appeared on the wall outside the principal's office. Only seniors were listed and not in alphabetical order. When one of us walked up to take a quick look, we wanted to send the message that we weren't checking out the academic rankings of our classmates. (We'd do that later when we were alone in the hallway.)

Senior-year conversations centered on which college we hoped to attend. As in previous years, we expected one to emerge with nearly universal appeal. This year was no different. For unknown reasons, the popular choice was Indiana University. Bloomington, Indiana, was 800 miles from Mount Vernon, New York.

***

None of the women in my family had yet applied to or attended college except for one great-aunt who had become a physician. But that exceptional woman had set such a high standard and she was considered an anomaly. Even in the 1940s, women doctors were rare.

Ma had graduated eighth grade and enrolled in business school. As valedictorian of her class, she was quick to find a job. Grandma had dressed her in a white shirtwaist and a dark skirt and pulled her hair back in a bun to mask her youth. She was only sixteen. "And," Ma always added, "I brought home the largest paycheck in the family."

Sylvia had completed the eighth grade and briefly attended vocational training at Lexington before Ma enrolled her in ninth grade at my junior high. But then Sylvia had found herself a job and formal education stopped until she took courses through a vocational rehabilitation program, which developed her bookkeeping proficiency.

Shirley attended Lexington until seventh grade and then transferred to a private school as the only deaf student. With the advantage of small class sizes and her teachers' support, she completed all requirements. From there, she attended a boarding school in Connecticut for one year, then graduated from Edgewood High School in Greenwich. Upon coursework completion at The Mount Vernon Business School, Shirley found employment with a bank, as a transit clerk. Late in life, Shirley told me that Ma's reluctance to have us far from home had stood in the way of her applying to Gallaudet.

Of my immediate family and all my girl cousins, I was the first—and for a long time the only—woman in our family who even considered going to college.

***

Months before I'd graduated from high school, I received a letter from Indiana University. I'd been accepted as a freshman starting September 1946.

My achievement didn't meet with enthusiasm at home. Ma had the idea that I should attend business school.

"But I want to go to college," I told her. "I don't want to be someone's secretary. How can you even think I'd want to study stenography and typing!"

"Then apply to New York University," she said. "It's closer to home. What could you possibly find in Indiana that you can't find right here?"

***

Out of Ma's presence, Sylvia who continued to live with her husband and baby in our family home, said, "She'll never let you go far away. Must control. Keep you nearby.

"Forget going out New York. Will never happen."

If I stayed home, it would not be to attend NYU. I had friends taking the train every morning to downtown New York and coming home laden with books. Their lives were about classes and commuting. They couldn't take part in any campus activity because of the commute.

Barnard College was a quick ride on the New York, New Haven, Hartford Railroad from Mount Vernon to Harlem, then a bus ride to campus. I weighed the reasons I liked Barnard: small classes, the opportunity to enroll in courses across the street at Columbia, one of the country's most prestigious universities, and it was close enough to home that I could stay late on campus before taking the train home. There would be no fights with Ma about going far away to school.

COLLEGE ACCEPTANCE

Grace Lewis was the assistant principal at A. B. Davis High School. She was tall and serious-looking with a frosty stare, and we students had little contact with her. When we did, we laughed at her pronouncements. For instance, she chastised us for not wearing socks with our sandals. She considered bare ankles an unnecessary provocation for the boys.

One day, she called my parents and me into her office. "I am concerned that Miriam has applied to Barnard College," she said. "It has a reputation for restricting its number of Jewish students. I would prefer she apply to Goucher College, from which I graduated. I know she would be accepted."

My parents were taken aback. I'd already been accepted at Indiana University and New York University. I already knew that neither Ma nor Daddy would agree to my going out of state. But this caused me to look at Miss Lewis in a new way. She cared. Behind that frosty demeanor and steely look, she cared.

"Well," Ma said, "we will give it some thought."

***

As a family, we never discussed the issue of anti-Semitism at Barnard College.

Within a few weeks, however, I was accepted at Barnard, although there wasn't enough room in the dorms for students who lived within commuting distance. I'd attend Barnard that fall but would continue to live at home.

BRANDEIS CAMP INSTITUTE, 1946

The summer before the start of my freshman year, my lifelong friend Margie and I were awarded scholarships to attend the Brandeis Camp Institute in the Pocono Mountains, a train and a bus ride away from home. Our local Zionist organization had selected us for that honor.

While eager to attend, all we knew for sure was that we'd experience kibbutz life, with daily routines similar to those in the Jewish settlements proliferating in Palestine. In our youth groups at home, we'd heard about this way of life and the attempts to bring Jewish refugees to Palestine.

As Margie and I entered the Brandeis campgrounds in the summer of 1946, we were struck by the sight of two flags, the Stars and Stripes of the United States of America and a blue flag we hoped would soon fly over what would become the State of Israel. Side by side, the flags fluttered at the tops of their flagpoles.

A kitchen-dining hall and a few other buildings dotted the campus. Our living quarters consisted of canvas tents surrounding the outdoor commons. Once we deposited our belongings onto our assigned cots, we gathered to stretch out on the grass. It was there we were introduced to camp founder and director Dr. Shlomo Bardin.

For the next month, all our activities were led by *shlichim,* Jewish emissaries who lived a kibbutz life in Palestine. If there was a job, it was ours to do. On a rotating basis, we worked the farm, ran the kitchen, attended classes, and led religious services.

Dr. Bardin met with a small group to discuss Jewish philosophers relevant to the camp's Zionist program. I was invited to join, and Dr. Bardin later invited me to be a youth speaker at the national convention of the Zionist Organization of America.

That fall, I shared my thoughts with a thousand-person conclave. Afterward, on my way to my hotel room, I waited for an elevator. A short distance away stood Anne Frank's father. I bowed my head.

LESSONS IN LEADERSHIP

It didn't take me long to step across the street from Barnard College to Columbia University. There I acquainted myself with Earl Hall and what that building provided to groups from both campuses. I began to attend meetings of the Intercollegiate Zionist Federation of America (IZFA).

Familiarity with the politics and purpose of Zionism, a common interest in the music of the Jewish diaspora, the sharing of experiences—along with the knowledge that some students planned on *aliyah*, a move to settle Palestine—captured me. IZFA on the Columbia campus became my new home.

Later that school year, two of us from Barnard, both brimming with optimism and innocence, made an appointment to meet Dean Virginia Gildersleeve. Dean Gildersleeve turned out to be the Barnard College dean my high school assistant vice principal had warned was anti-Semitic. At our meeting, we explained our wish to have an IZFA chapter on our campus, one developed and led by Barnard women. We hoped for her expressed approval.

"You probably do not know this," she said, "but I am the national secretary of the Arab American Friendship League. I am opposed to everything that IZFA stands for."

Not knowing what to say next, my friend and I looked at each other uncertainly.

"However," said the dean, "you have every right to espouse your point of view on this campus. I will provide a charter for your group."

The dean had taught us a lesson, one that would affect our thinking for the rest of our lives: Broaden the conversation, learn about differences, and don't assume only one way is right.

LIFE OR DEATH CHOICES

There was something relaxing about our family's grocery shopping at the end of each week. Daddy would park the car and use the steering wheel to prop up whatever book he was reading as he waited for Ma and me to return. Ma and I would get coffee and a sweet at the bake shop before we began to shop.

This Sunday was different. Daddy parked the car in front of Chester's Chicken Store, but as I opened the car door to step out, Ma said, "Just a minute. Daddy wants to say something."

Without turning to face me, Daddy said, "If you ever marry a man with hearing loss, I will commit suicide."

"And he means it," said Ma. "We know what you are up to in New York. We know who you are dating."

How foolish. Of course. The deaf world is close-knit. Dating anyone considered part of that world, no matter how casual the relationship, would be noted and shared. It didn't even matter how Daddy and Ma had found out.

Nothing was private, welcome, or normal. Nothing. Why was Daddy so against my marrying a deaf man? Was Daddy afraid I might give birth to a deaf child, a grandchild with whom he wouldn't be able to talk?

***

I remembered when Daddy was my first movie date. The movie title comes from one of its songs. *Alexander's Ragtime Band.* Daddy sings to me. The movie ends and I want to stay. "But they're going to show it all over again," I cry. "But it's time to go home," Daddy says. "But it's going to show again," I insist. "Not for us," says Uncle Eddie, who is at the movie with Daddy and me, ". . . for the people who haven't seen it yet."

Thereafter, whenever Daddy and I made our way home from the movies, he'd hum the remnants of songs we'd heard. Sometimes he sang the words off-key, and I'd join in. Word for word, I'd copy his off-key tune.

At home, he'd sing songs heard on the radio. *You're the cream in my coffee! . . . You're the apple of my eye!* And I'd interpret the words for Sylvia and then for Shirley because neither could lipread Daddy. No matter how they tried, my sisters could not understand what Daddy said. Ma could convey what Daddy was saying if asked, but if neither Ma nor I was there, Daddy had limited communication with his two deaf daughters, although through his own doing.

Was this his life's abiding sorrow? Was he fearful that his fate would be my fate?

***

Smiling Daddy. Sweet Daddy. I'd always go to Daddy with my questions because he gave me more answers than Ma. But how did my sisters see him? When I asked, they said Daddy was sweet. He was kind. He was quiet, while Ma was strict.

Whether Daddy chose to end his life or not depended on the choices I made in my own life. What was I to do with my new burden? Could I live my own life and remain the apple of Daddy's eye?

DR. ALSOP

As a day college student, I'd continued seeing our family doctor. But now, with the problem I had, I couldn't go to him. My trust in him had ruptured when I'd broken my leg and he'd shown me no concern. I needed to talk to someone I could trust. Also, I needed to talk with someone not connected to my family. I had to tell someone what was bothering me.

I was given an appointment with Dr. Gulielma Alsop. Dr. Alsop had founded the Medical Department at Barnard College and headed it until her retirement fifty-two years later.

"What brings you here this morning?" she asked. In her white medical coat, hair brushed behind her ears, she looked stern, all business.

"I need to figure something out. My life is all mixed up between hearing and deaf people."

"What do you mean?"

I described my family and friends in the deaf community. How I was often referred to as, "You know, Miriam Hearing Sister, the girl with two deaf sisters." And out it poured. What Daddy had said. Daddy, wearing his two hearing aids, not facing me. Daddy . . . so gentle. Daddy, who'd taught me the escape and rescue that reading delivers. Daddy . . . to whom I could talk with about anything—except this. I couldn't move beyond what Daddy had said.

Dr. Alsop sat back in her chair.

"I have a suggestion," she said. "I have a dorm room, over which I have control. I may use it for students whom I feel would benefit from living away from home. I think you need time to think through your relationships with your family."

She continued, "You may have that dorm room through this year. Then, at the end of the year, you can go through the regular dorm application process. Let me know tomorrow whether you'd like to do this."

"Yes. I do want a change. I'll speak with my parents this evening. I'll let you know tomorrow."

She'd listened. She'd heard me. She understood what I needed.

LEAVING HOME

That evening, as Ma fixed dinner and Daddy stood at the kitchen counter with the receptor of his hearing aid pressed against the radio, I waited as he listened to the news. I waited for us to sit down, as Daddy had his shot of schnapps, and as Ma moved from counter to stove to fill our plates.

Shirley was away at school. Sylvia and Carl were upstairs having dinner in their own small kitchen on the third floor. I jumped in. "I heard something at school today. There is a room available for this year in the dorm and it's been offered to me."

"Live at school?" asked Ma.

"Like all my friends from high school who went away to college. Like Margie, who's at Cincinnati. Like Henrie, who's at Indiana. Like I would have done if I weren't going to Barnard. Because . . ." The look on Ma's face stopped me from saying more. Daddy was sitting tall in his chair, but leaning forward, his hand placed on his hearing aid controls. I tried again, softly cushioning with bland generalities my reason for leaving.

"Living at home is just like going to high school, except I take a train instead of walk. . . .Everyone leaves home at some time. I'm eighteen. It's my time to live with other girls in a dorm that's well supervised." Ma looked at me expressionlessly.

"Look," I asserted, "Sylvia lived in the dorms at school. Shirley lives at school now."

"That's different," Ma said. "There's no school here for them. They had to live away from home during the week."

Daddy looked at me and then at Ma. But he said nothing.

I'd used all the words I knew to appease Ma's insecurities about orderliness, naturalness, and inevitability. My voice broke. "I need to be away! It's my time to be with friends—my classmates. I would only be around the corner. I'd be just a subway ride away. Please. I need this."

"How much will it cost?" Ma asked.

Facts in a row, I answered.

Ma turned to Daddy. "Well?"

"Now?" he asked.

"Now," I answered.

Ma and Daddy looked at each other and then at me. They nodded.

"Well," said Ma, "you can try it for this year. We'll see how it goes."

I went upstairs to my room, spread out on my bed, and cried. I'd remembered Ma saying to one of her relatives, "It's so nice having Miriam here. She can hear me."

FINDING MY PLACE IN THE WORLD

I moved into the dorm the next week on a Sunday morning. We packed the car with my clothes, books, desk lamp, typewriter, and bedsheets for the dorm bed. Shirley climbed in the backseat with me and I explained I was going to live at school, just like she lived at Lexington.

"Dorm . . . like Lexington?" she asked. "Come home on weekends?"

"No. Stay at school. Go to library. Study hard."

"But I miss you," she said, getting teary-eyed.

"I have an idea. Your school's not far from mine. I'll come to your school sometimes in the afternoons, and we will go to Bloomingdale's." Her face brightened. Bloomingdale's was my eleven-year-old sister's favorite stop. "We'll ride the escalators," I said, "and the perfume ladies will spray perfume on our wrists." And that's exactly what we did.

In the meantime, we carried everything into the front door of my girls' dorm while Daddy got permission to go upstairs. Without permission, no males, including fathers, were permitted beyond the reception area.

With my floormates pitching in, it took little time for us to carry everything upstairs. Ma looked around and said, "It looks like a cell."

My cell, I thought. *It is my cell. Mine.*

***

When Ma and Daddy left to take Shirley back to Lexington, I made my bed, placed my typewriter on the desk, hung my clothes, and folded the rest inside a dresser drawer.

I was listening to the quiet when I heard a distant radio, then laughter coming from the hallway. New sounds for me. I walked out and found my classmates. They invited me to join them in one of their rooms. Like all the other dorm rooms, the room was small, too small to have chairs for everyone. I sat on the floor and entered, completely, into what Daddy wanted—my place in the hearing world.

Part Eight

The Truth about Deaf Babies

MY TRADE

Like many mothers of that era, Ma would smile and say, "I hope you are going for an M R S (Mrs.) degree." But Daddy always said, "You must have a trade. You never know what can happen in life. You must have a way to take care of yourself."

Barnard College offered me that pathway. But in the meantime, I took an elective in Bible with Dr. Ursula Niebuhr. As requested, we arrived with colored pencils and a copy of the Old Testament. We'd been told we'd be coloring a path through the chapters, designating by color the presumed author of each verse.

Our professor introduced herself by stating she didn't speak a foreign language, as prior students had complained, but in time, we'd adjust to her British accent. I studied with Dr. Niebuhr for several semesters. Along with other students, I accepted invitations to her home at Union Theological Seminary where her husband, the esteemed scholar Reinhold Niebuhr, was a professor.

Still, I knew that religious studies wouldn't be my trade.

***

I began my studies in the sociology department. Professor Conrad Arensburg taught us about communities, and I embarked on a months-long study of Mount Vernon. My home community was embroiled in planning for the site of a new high school. I met with the head of the NAACP. As he drove me across our city, he indicated how the proposed location for the new school ignored the lack of transportation for Black students. I also met with parents whose children attended the academic high school. They were concerned that money would be siphoned from academics to enhance the new school's vocational courses.

Perhaps, with my love of books and research, a doctorate in sociology was in the offing, but what about a trade? I began to think about social work. It attracted me to direct intervention with individuals who needed counseling services. And that could be my trade.

Besides, graduate school would keep me in an academic environment, which I loved.

LETTER FROM LEN

Ma and Daddy had accustomed themselves to my parade of boyfriends, which included old friends from high school and students from Columbia. There had even been an attempt by a great-aunt (the physician) to introduce me to a patient's son. That was a disaster. Throughout it all, Daddy came to remark, "Miriam loves them all, but only one at a time."

In the summer of 1949, Bob (my date to my high school senior prom) was home from college, and we became reacquainted through the Mount Vernon Round Table, a discussion group led by a Unitarian minister and his wife. Bob and I headed out to dance and have a beer at the popular Glen Island Casino. In the fall, Bob returned to Baltimore for his senior year at Johns Hopkins University. Not long after, I received a letter from his good friend Len.

11 October 1949

Dear Mim,

Thought you might be interested in how the other half lives — that is, the other half that your man, Bob, tries, unsuccessfully, to make livable. First, may I bow low from the waist as a matter of American custom and, secondly, extend my hand for a friendly handshake.

Yes, Bob was a bit changed from when I saw him last in June — I don't think it is the fact that it was 1:15 a.m. when I awakened him, but rather the fact, as he explained to me later, that he had met you during the summer. I believe that it's grand and I hope your futures crystallize as planned.

When do you plan [sic] coming down here? I'm sure that Bob will make your stay a pleasant one. It was grand "meeting" you and I hope to see you soon.

Sincerely,

Len

A SERIOUS BOYFRIEND

Bob's reentry into my life led me to acknowledge to myself, "He's nice. Bright. Comes from a good family." I said nothing more. By the time I graduated from college, Bob was a part of my life and my family's life, spending time in our home and commandeering the store register during the Christmas rush.

Ma and Daddy were more than pleased. Relieved. It looked like Miriam finally had made her choice. Yet, still clutching to my independence, I shared a few of my feelings for Bob with my family. I sought every opportunity to travel to see him in Baltimore.

Once we'd graduated college, we both moved on to graduate school—Bob at Hopkins Medical School in Baltimore and me at the Columbia School of Social Work in New York City.

Bob's med school roommate, also named Bob, had a girlfriend in New York City. On weekends, she and I took the train to Baltimore together. When the boys moved out of their one-room apartment, we girls moved in. Marion's presence assuaged Ma's worry about the propriety of those long-distance visits.

DAMAGED GOODS

One weekend in Baltimore, after nearly two years of steady dating, Bob surprised me with an engagement ring.

Ma had insisted I go to Baltimore, even though I'd fallen and hurt my ankle that Friday morning. She'd rushed me to a radiologist who diagnosed a sprained ankle and sent me on my way with a cane. Bob had let my parents in on the surprise. He'd also arranged for the two of us to meet his father for dinner. Dr. Zadek was in Baltimore for a medical conference. At dinner, his congratulations belied what was to come. I soon heard of his inquiries of doctors who'd treated Daddy at one time or another for a variety of concerns. Various possibilities were offered for Daddy's hearing loss, but Bob's father had one underlying question: If Bob and I conceived a child, what were the risks that our child would be born deaf?

Four days before our wedding, Bob's father convinced his stepson from his second marriage to speak with Bob—to urge Bob that he still had time to divest of his marital obligation to me.

***

Bob and I married on June 15, 1952. I danced with his father at the wedding reception. Bob's father was at least willing to dance with the bride he considered damaged goods.

STARTING A FAMILY

As the time approached for Bob to complete medical school, we started talking about having children. Saying nothing of this to our parents, we made an appointment at McKusick-Nathans Institute of Genetic Medicine in Baltimore. Our questions for the geneticist focused on whether or not we should expect a deaf child.

The possibility that our child would be born deaf wouldn't deter us, but it would bring into focus immediate decisions having to do with our relocation for Bob's upcoming surgical training and his surgical practice. If our child was born deaf, we'd need to decide what approach we would embrace—whether we would, as my parents had, choose oralism. Or would we adopt a more encompassing approach, using all avenues for communication, including sign language. There was research to do. My older sister Sylvia, who was now in her thirties, and her husband had enrolled their son Philip in Lexington School, a school that still restricted itself to the oral language approach. But there were other schools that gave less attention to oral language and lipreading, focusing primarily on teaching and communication through sign language.

Our young doctor was forthcoming and enthusiastic. He understood that the only deaf histories we could provide were those of my younger and older sisters, their husbands, and my nephew and niece. Sherry, Sylvia's second child, had been born that previous March.

Charts were formulated based on the information we provided. The doctor said our chances of having a deaf child were remote, so we put aside the need to plan for a deaf child.

WHEN THINGS GO WRONG

Our first child was born at Duke University Hospital in Durham, North Carolina, where Bob was amid a surgical internship. The road that fronted our apartment led to Duke. Duke's obstetrical service was among the first to offer a "modification" for natural childbirth: an analgesia called Trilene.

To learn what to expect during labor, I attended child birthing classes. Useful breathing techniques were emphasized, and care was given to never use the word "pain." Preferred words included "pressure" and "straining." Of course, when the pressure became intense, there was a modification: the Trilene mask. The mask was held by the patient so that she could self-administer a whiff of comfort when necessary.

After Bob found me poring over his obstetrics textbook, learning about the major complications and consequences of childbirth when a delivery didn't go as planned, he took the book to the hospital. Shortly thereafter, I offered up his pediatric textbook for there, too, I'd found examples of the more extreme outcomes of pregnancy.

I didn't bother to examine the textbook section on pediatric deafness.

THE TRUTH ABOUT DEAF BABIES

Sarah was born one morning in February. A routine labor preceded a normal delivery, and there she was, black-haired and brown-eyed, weighing seven pounds and three ounces.

At that time, it was customary for the mother and baby to remain in the hospital for five days. This was to receive assistance in breastfeeding, diapering, and burping the baby. There were also classes for the new mothers and visits from the pediatric house staff.

Our pediatrician arrived the day that Sarah and I were to come home. He checked the baby's reflexes, looked into her eyes, peered into her ears, and asked me how the breastfeeding was going. The doctor waited as I dressed Sarah in her first outfit, a pink infant dress, complete with slip and hand-knit pink sweater and cap.

"Doctor," I asked, "can you test the baby's hearing?"

"Why would that be necessary?" he asked.

"My family history," I reminded him. "My sisters are deaf. My niece and nephew are deaf."

Ignoring my response, he replied, "She's a beautiful baby," as he walked out of the room.

That much I knew already.

A GIFT FROM MY SISTERS

When Bob and I returned to Baltimore three years later from North Carolina by way of Norfolk, Virginia, we returned with our first two little girls, Sarah and Susan. Bob had completed his internship at Duke Hospital followed by a stint in the U.S. Navy. Beth and then Barbara were yet to be born.

Bob immediately started his surgical residency at Johns Hopkins, and I returned part-time to clinical social work at the Child Study Center, a residential treatment center for emotionally disturbed children in Baltimore. I'd worked there full-time before Bob's internship at Duke.

Upon my return, one of my first client families had at its center a nonverbal, unresponsive, fearful, six-year-old boy. Most parents would find such behaviors disturbing. It is unusual and exceedingly difficult, and painful, to have a child who appears so untrusting and is so disconnected. Decades of counseling parents in both private and group settings would teach me this.

To begin therapy, we started with the parents. We took a history, assisted the parents in understanding what could be going on with the child, and worked with them on their feelings and issues that were sometimes unrelated to the little boy.

Each day that the little boy entered my office, he walked past me and avoided looking in my direction. He immediately climbed into my desk keyhole, curling up and settling in where the desk chair would sit. I hummed softly. We spent many minutes that way. One day I went to the keyhole to sit with him. Both of us under the desk—not touching—I continued to hum and then said his name. After several weeks of this, I felt it was time to stay in my chair. The boy moved out from the empty space under the desk and—still not looking at me—crawled onto my lap.

The boy was trusting me a little more. By allowing him space, and only by entering into the next phase when he gave the signal, I used many ways to develop a connection with the boy that eventually allowed us to communicate.

Communicating was so much a part of my private and professional life. How natural for me. How intuitive. This was a gift from my sisters—seek out ways, all ways, to communicate.

MA AS MY ROLE MODEL

Helen Keller and Polly Thompson (Anne Sullivan's successor) sit waiting to the right of where Ma stands at the podium. As the prime mover of the school's parents' group, Ma did everything from bringing parental concerns to the attention of the school's superintendent to setting out chairs for meetings and inviting guest speakers.

This night, every seat in the Hunter College auditorium was taken. While none of the Lexington parents had a DeafBlind child, Helen Keller and her teacher-companion, Anne Sullivan, had achieved more than most anyone had thought possible.

Reflecting on this, I consider Ma and all that she did for my sisters and me. Though we'd seen Ma as overprotective and controlling, it was her assertiveness that allowed her daughters to step out into the world prepared. She'd raised all three of us to have guts, to be daughters who'd help pave the way for others.

I only began to understand this as I started to fashion my own role in the world; yes, I did find assertiveness necessary when answering the call for *tikkun olam*—the call to repair the world.

MY LIFE'S WORK

At Barnard, I'd developed a special interest in populations in need. When Bob and I returned to Baltimore from Durham with our growing family, I applied for three jobs and was offered all three. My choice had been an easy one: the residential treatment center for children. For children considered out of the ordinary.

Moving on, I initiated a social work program at Children's Hospital in Baltimore (now part of the Johns Hopkins Hospital), with the opportunity to train graduate social workers from the University of Maryland. I also had an appointment at the University of Maryland's School of Dentistry to work with dental students, sensitizing them to the psychosocial challenges children might experience as a result of oral-facial anomalies. I began a counseling support group for parents.

In 1975, the Hearing and Speech Agency (HASA) of Metropolitan Baltimore called. They had received a federal grant to develop a model program for intervention with families and children who had "communicative disorders." Even though I'd planned to take the summer off, they offered to pay me over the summer to "just read," as long as they could put my name on the grant as the social worker who would develop a service model.

I agreed, and I enrolled in a series of audiology courses. Such courses were not required for my new social work position, but I felt that the additional knowledge would be beneficial when, on the behalf of parents, I consulted with the other professionals on our team.

CONTINUING MY STUDIES

The antique hearing aid in my hand was cumbersome, bulky, and it was exactly like the body aid my father wore. I'd never held Daddy's aid in my hand, for Ma would not have permitted it. "*Not for you.*" I could hear her words now as if the very act of holding the aid against my ear would cause me to be deaf.

I recalled how Daddy's aid had weighed down his shirt pocket. Slowly lifting the earpiece, holding it against my ear, I turned its dial just as I remembered Daddy doing. I heard my instructor's voice—thin, tinny, a poor imitation of how her voice sounded to me. When a student asked a question, a skeletal copy of that student's voice came through.

Handing the aid to the student on my right, I had a sudden and sorrowful realization. Engrossed in my studies, learning about the structure and functioning of the human ear, there was something the books or any lecture did not reveal.

No matter the resonance of my voice, no matter if it was filled with passion or sadness, what Daddy had heard was a filtered, metallic recital. My father had only known my voice in this tinny, artificial way; he never knew how I really sounded. In this particular and essential way of my being, I had remained unknown to him.

My classmates would never know the sense of loss I felt at that moment.

PARENTS AND CHILD: TO UNDERSTAND, TO BE UNDERSTOOD

After years of clinical social work experience followed by studies in audiology, I arrived, as agreed, at HASA for that federal grant. Children enrolled in the HASA school program had a variety of conditions that influenced their ability to express or understand speech. Many were deaf or hard of hearing. For some kids, acquisition of speech required sequential steps like using two- or three-word phrases or understanding the names of things. Once parents could be helped to recognize this, it set a better dynamic between parent and child.

When a parent wanted a child to receive counseling I worked privately with that child, but the backbone of the social work program was for parents.

***

I worked for two decades at HASA. Five parents came for a weekly meeting. One returned to the group with her new baby, who was cradled in a carrier. The mother set the carrier at her feet as we made ourselves comfortable on the sofa and chairs. All eyes were on the baby. She wiggled, stretched her arms, kicked her tiny feet, and moved her face from side to side. As we dwelled on this little miracle, sweet murmurings arose from the circle of mothers.

I said, "Just look at us! We can't take our eyes off her! How enchanting a new baby is. We stop everything . . . I wonder how it must feel to be the older kid?"

This question was all that was needed for the discussion. Talk turned to a child's place in the family, the way there is sometimes ambivalence with changes in family roles and responsibilities. A grandmother in the group talked about "mother wit," how she'd raised her children and taken responsibility for the grandchild in our program at HASA.

Sharing her store of wisdom about what went well, what problems she and her family were working to overcome, the parents and therapist listened. As we shared problems and solutions, we learned from each other. We built that healing bond that comes from trust and support.

PAYING IT FORWARD: THE INTERPRETER SERVICE

One day HASA received a call from the Baltimore Council on Aging. For years, the council had provided funding in support of housing for deaf residents, but it was now considering the prospect of moving those funds to a new initiative. They invited us to submit a proposal.

A nonprofit interpreting service could be an important initiative for the Baltimore Metropolitan Area, I thought. I knew what happened when deaf people were excluded from rightful places in the community. Jury duty, for example, wasn't an option without an interpreter. The lack of an interpreter when a deaf person was hospitalized could become a catastrophic problem.

We'd recently received an urgent call from a hospital. A deaf patient had been diagnosed with HIV, and hospital personnel felt they could explain the diagnosis. But following the discussion, the patient attempted suicide. When an interpreter arrived at the hospital, a grim misperception was untangled. The patient hadn't understood that he didn't have AIDS, that his diagnosis of HIV could be controlled.

The need for an interpreter at hospitals and when consulting with physicians is not that unusual. I also had personal awareness of where the medical system had failed in this way. A relative, a hearing woman with a deaf husband, ran into difficulty during labor, yet she was expected to interpret what was going on for her husband. The hospital was successfully sued.

In 1986, our proposal for the area's first nonprofit ASL interpreting service agency was funded. The task to raise the rest of the money began. I approached friends who provided the additional funds. We were on our way.

As it turned out, the need for interpreters was so great that the Centralized Interpreter Referral Service (CIRS) was soon bringing in 50 percent of HASA's annual income. More than three decades later, CIRS continues to thrive. The program now provides not only interpreters but also training for new interpreters.

This reminds me of an experience informing the importance of interpreters educated in specialized areas. Several years ago, I was at a meeting where I met a new teacher, an instructor in physics at a local public school I asked him how it was going.

"Awful!" he replied. He then told me a story. A deaf student came into his physics class the first day of classes, accompanied by a sign language interpreter who said, "I don't know how I can help. I don't have the skill set to interpret physics." In addition, the teacher discovered that the student, entering tenth grade, had only a second-grade reading level. The school system had pushed him along without addressing it.

As the nation has moved toward integrating deaf students into mainstream classrooms, how often are their needs addressed in an adequate way?

Part Nine

First Language

NOT QUITE FORGOTTEN

Upon holding his infant granddaughter for the first time, Bob's father shook his keys and handed her back to me when she didn't wake up.

"I see no evidence that this child hears," he said and turned away. My heart dropped. I saw nothing of the happiness I'd expected him to feel at the birth of his first grandchild.

Only as I write these words does the sting return.

***

Ten days after the death of Bob's stepmother, Bob's father died in our home.

He was ninety years old and had expressed to us that he had no wish to continue living. I took leave from work to stay home with him. I read him poetry and he recited his favorite poems to me. Many times he returned to "Invictus" by William Ernest Henley. *Out of the night that covers me, Black as the pit from pole to pole, I thank whatever gods may be . . . For my unconquerable soul. . . . In the fell clutch of circumstance . . . Beyond this place of wrath and tears . . . Finds and shall find me unafraid. . . . It matters not how strait the gate, How charged with punishments the scroll, I am the master of my fate, I am the captain of my soul.* Henley had written that poem when he was in the hospital being treated for tuberculosis of the bone.

I thought about how this poem reflected his personality and life. My husband saw his father as a man with many strong opinions. He was a very smart man who viewed life with few areas of gray, and he rarely changed his mind. We'd had moments of disconnection and pain over the years, but also moments of connection.

A BROKEN SILENCE

It was a fall morning when Bob and I were driving back to Baltimore from Rehoboth in Delaware, and I asked a question. We'd shared a long weekend with friends, attended a meeting, hosted a book club dinner, and then relaxed on our porch. From there we could hear the Atlantic crash on a beach then deserted. The next morning, our niece Sherry and her husband Andy had joined us for breakfast at Crystal, our usual haunt. Perhaps something in our conversation had caused certain thoughts to resurface on the car ride home.

"Bob," I asked, "if our first child had been deaf, how would you have felt about having a second child?"

"Maybe not four kids," he responded, "but sure, we would have had more kids."

I remembered how we'd consulted with a Hopkins geneticist as we'd planned our first baby. Before our first baby came into the world, we felt the need to make a decision. If the doctor had told us our child would be born deaf, it would have affected our choice of state and city in which to live, as location could limit or broaden our options to educate our deaf child. But the physician had reassured us that the possibility of our having a deaf child was slim. So our concerns about moving had diminished.

I remembered Bob's father asking me to ride with him on an errand. "I want you to know," he said, "I am hoping that your marriage to Bob will dissolve." I'd been stunned into silence. Until that moment, many years later, I'd never told Bob what had been said.

Bob asked why I'd never told him. I explained that he was close to his father and that the father-son relationship held meaning. Bob knew that his father had vigorously opposed our marriage, and while I'd hoped that his father's opposition would be erased by the fact that Bob and I had married, it had not. My choice had been either to provoke a rupture between Bob and his father or to simply stay silent.

Bob thanked me. My decision had allowed him to maintain a relationship with his father.

REMAINDERS

What are the effects of my growing up hearing in a deaf world?
I touch people to get their attention before I speak.
When I raise a question, my eyebrows lift, my chin tilts forward.
I read lips.

***

I lipread in both worlds, deaf and hearing. Sometimes I get caught in the act of catching information or confidences that don't belong to me. I feel uneasy not seeing a speaker's face. Even when I may not be aware of what I'm doing, I maneuver from behind the speaker to watch the speaker's face, to follow the words as they form on the speaker's lips. Even though I once had perfect hearing, lipreading reassured me.

When I want someone's attention, I touch that person's shoulder or gently rest my hand on her arm before I speak. It isn't enough for me to say someone's name before I begin. My deaf community has told me that my gestures and expressions are deaf-like.

***

Growing up it wasn't necessary to project my voice—except when talking with Daddy. With Ma, I could speak to her from any room, and she would answer back. Whatever was said, we knew we were the only ones to hear.

***

For too many years, in almost every encounter, when an inability to communicate with someone—anyone—led to disagreement and anger, I felt I'd caused it. It fell on me to make certain the situation ended amicably.

GENETIC TESTING

My sisters and I had married and raised our children before scientists had even begun to publicly report on the discovery of a mutated gene and its link to hereditary deafness. Although there are more than 400 genes, this one was of interest to me.

In the late 1990s, my niece Sherry informed me that Gallaudet University and the Medical College of Virginia were collaborating to test individuals for the presence of the GJB2 gene mutation, which was responsible for the insufficient production of the Connexin 26 protein, the most common cause of genetic deafness in Ashkenazi Jews among others.

By that time, I had four daughters and ten grandchildren, all hearing. But what might my genes foretell? Was I a carrier, a conduit for future generations? My memory of Ma and Daddy's anguish resonated. *But Miriam can hear.* And there was that question always set at Ma's feet, always that same question. *There's no deafness in our families. . . . And, in your case?*

Most hearing parents who give birth to deaf babies are caught unaware. It's certainly better to be prepared for such a possibility. That was why Bob and I had sought genetic counseling before our first child was conceived. Deaf or hearing, we knew we wanted a child, but we also understood the need to prepare, to make good decisions.

Where would we find the best opportunity for educating a deaf child? What audiological evaluations would be needed? Where could we obtain American Sign Language instruction? And, most important, which of the current teaching philosophies would we adopt for our family? We felt our family's future rested in the balance of preparing for such contingencies.

In 2000, I contacted Gallaudet and was included in the protocol. A year later, the results arrived. Both my niece and her brother's son, my great-nephew, carry the mutated gene.

Further data indicated the strong likelihood that both my parents carried a recessive mutation in the GJB2 gene. Ma and Daddy had had a one in four chance of having a hearing child.

I was that kid. I did not carry the recessive mutation. I was seventy when I received this information and was startled by it. Perhaps if we had known this earlier, it would have eased the reaction of Bob's parents to our marriage. This was information for my grandchildren and their progeny.

LOCATING THE EAST: OUR GENETIC FAMILY TREE

A cousin who came from Shanghai immediately post-WWII did some work on developing a family tree. He found that my father had a deaf aunt who perished in the Holocaust.

It was only by accident we found each other. A travel article published on the internet came to the attention of a man whose father was described in the article as having come to the United States from Shanghai after WWII. The man discovered that I had written the piece and asked for a copy. I answered his email: "Dear Cousin, I was at your parents' wedding."

And so, it began. Yehuda was Daddy's second cousin living in Brooklyn. We shared family information and he sent me the family tree he'd compiled. Five generations of my father's forebears were included.

In turn, and over time, I provided my newly found cousin with subsequent generations of my family and of my sisters' families. Our ancestral tree now documents ten generations of family. Then, together with my sisters' children, we developed genetic family trees. Starting with Ma and Daddy, each tree documents five generations. Noted are those who are hearing and those who are deaf.

Our lack of genetic knowledge of earlier generations is notable. This is largely because my father's ties to extended family were severed when his widowed mother brought him to this country as a young boy—and how fortunate that she did. From Yehuda, I learned that close relatives perished in the Pinsk Ghetto in 1942.

FIRST LANGUAGE

Though my children are hearing, as are their children and grandchildren, it makes me smile to see one of my granddaughters using sign language to communicate with her infant daughter. As if to explain to me, she said, "Sign is the first language with which children can begin to communicate."

The book from which she selected appropriate signs was a gift to her from my niece Sherry. A book on infant sign language would be one of the first gifts I'd give to my two great-granddaughters.

***

I remember my nephew Harvey, Shirley's younger son, telling me he'd learned nothing until he transferred from an oral school to one where sign language was used. My niece Sherry told me of her early experiences at Lexington, the hearing dorm counselors were "impossible to lipread," and, instead of using ASL, each counselor created her own crude gestures.

***

One day not long ago, a great-nephew watched as my niece, Sherry, and I conversed orally. He turned to her and, in ASL, asked how she did that. She explained, "I know how to lipread." I asked the reason for the boy's question and his grandfather explained that if the child can't speak with a clear voice, the boy's school's speech pathologists don't consider lipreading an option.

***

As defined by each child's needs, at HASA I'd embraced all options, but I especially understood the importance of sign language exposure for deaf children. My mother was deeply influenced by the oralist methods of teaching deaf children that were so prevalent in the 1920s. I have no memory of her considering any method other than that used at Lexington which was oralism. Though she did accept the use of sign language as the appropriate way for Sylvia and Shirley to communicate with each other and their friends, she kept them focused on communicating orally with the hearing, because the hearing world was largely ignorant of sign language.

While I acquired some sign language skills on the sly, certainly, I was the beneficiary of my sisters' willingness to communicate orally with me. I had no problem understanding their speech. With limited sign, gesture, and their ability to lipread, we were able to communicate.

A LOVELY DAY

I sat on a bench
in the London Park
and watched

The man signed
as he offered his son
milk

Simple signs

The child shook his
hand
fist closed
signing "yes"

Pardon me, I said,
I have a deaf family, I noticed your sign

Oh, the man said,
he's not deaf
both our kids go to nursery
where sign is used
before speech kicks in

For all kids

TODAY'S DIFFERENT WORLD

My TTY (teletypewriter) is consigned to the attic inside a box with other artifacts—a compact device once used to receive and deliver messages over the phone to and from deaf friends and family.

A great-nephew, living in the West, comes to meet us at the beach along the eastern shore. With the Cardzilla app, developed by a Deaf person, we converse with ease. He moves from one family member to another, exchanging cordialities and initiating conversations about spouses and children, and careers.

***

"Look at the family," says my husband of nearly seventy years, "college graduates with master's degrees from universities, executives at deaf schools and in major corporations, like Sprint and IBM, serving as board chairs at Gallaudet and Lexington Center. And all moving in directions both within the deaf community and the hearing community."

Certainly, the enactment of the Americans with Disabilities Act (ADA) in 1992 enhanced opportunities for our deaf relatives. The availability of both interpreter services and relay call systems has further opened communications between deaf and hearing people.

***

A story my older sister told me decades ago: For many years, she worked as a bookkeeper for the PepsiCo Corporation. One day, her supervisor commented, "Sylvia, if you could hear, you would have my job."

Sylvia answered, "If I could hear, I would be a pediatrician."

And today that would be possible, as evidenced by the many deaf doctors working around the nation.

***

I watch as all the children and their grandchildren move about, finding careers that appreciate their skill sets and offer rewarding opportunities.

My mother, who lived until her ninety-ninth year, constantly expressed amazement at what my nieces and nephews accomplished. My father did not live to witness this progress. Every now and then, I wonder how Daddy would have felt. Might he have been reassured if he could have seen the promise of tomorrow? I know that my mother, who lived longer, treasured each achievement.

As do I.

IN THE YEAR 2022

Seek to learn constantly while you live,
do not wait in the faith that old age by itself will bring wisdom.
– SOLON

My little sister Shirley (age 86) and I (age 93) remain in frequent contact. When I telephone Shirley using the federally funded video relay service, an interpreter comes on the line to say, "I am dialing the number now and will let you know when we connect."

Within moments, the call connects. Shirley signs via video to the interpreter who then speaks into the phone. "Hello, this is Shirley. Who is this?"

I answer. "Hi, Sis! It's Miriam. Can we chat a little? How are you doing?"

Our conversations take a familiar path.

I now have some age-related hearing loss and know what it is like to feel my face wrinkling with effort as if it would help me hear better. I smile as I recall what my sisters and I called the "deaf smile," describing situations where a smile was the only appropriate response: A person talked too quickly for lipreading, a sister didn't have enough interest or time to ask the speaker to repeat, or an interpreter couldn't be found.

Shirley has two sons, both deaf, five deaf grandchildren, and seven great-grandchildren, six of whom are deaf.

My older sister, Sylvia, had two children, both deaf. Her son Phil (Ma's first grandchild) has three deaf children and is grandfather to four deaf children and four hearing children. Sylvia's daughter Sherry has two sons, both hearing, and four grandchildren, all hearing. One daughter-in-law is deaf.

Bob and I have four daughters, eleven grandchildren, and six great-grandchildren, all hearing.

Our joys are mixed with stumbles along the way, sometimes retrievable, sometimes not, but I can now understand that these stumbles are merely a part of living. We take pleasure in our successes and, more importantly, forgive ourselves for what we might regret.

Everyone's path is strewn with stones. We learn to step around them. From my parents, I learned to step with optimism, confront barriers, and be an instrument for the elimination of obstacles.

Might our family life have been different, *fuller,* had we used the entire complement of options—ASL, hearing aids, oral language, and lipreading? It seems likely. . . . Even my minimal expertise in sign language gave me valuable access to my sisters and their world. And being an important cog in their lives as Miriam Hearing Sister was just as valuable to me as it was to them.

I was fortunate. I lived my life in both worlds.

> *Between stimulus and response lies a space.*
> *In that space lie our freedom and power to choose a response.*
> *In our response lies our growth and our happiness.*
>
> attributed to VIKTOR FRANKL

Sometimes, inadvertently, the space opens and we enter it, reflexively, because it is the only and the right way to go.

FAMILY PHOTOGRAPHS

Phil Bravin and Sherry Duhon's families. Sylvia's children, Phil (left of center) and Sherry (right), reunite with Aunt Miriam and Uncle Bob at Rehoboth Beach, Del. Annual summer gatherings since 1993 have included four generations of family.

Sunshine and ocean air. Daddy (Mr. H. I.) and Ma (Mrs. Scharfman)

No school day. Shirley, age thirteen

Getting around; Sylvia, age fifteen

Wedding day; Miriam and Bob, June 15, 1952

Four girls. Parents, Miriam and Bob, with their young daughters (left to right): Susan, Beth, Barb, and Sarah

Four grown daughters. Bob and Miriam (center), with Susan, Beth, Barb, and Sarah (left to right)

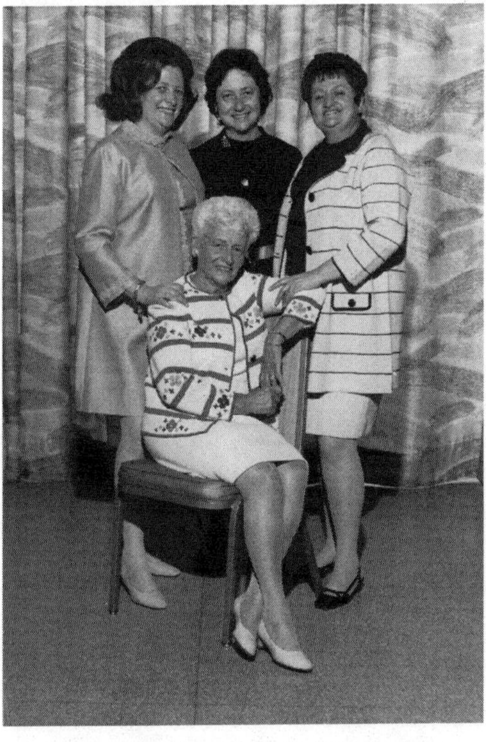

Ma and her daughters. Frances (Saffer) Scharfman with (left to right) Sylvia, Miriam, and Shirley

Zadek grandchildren

Shirley and Wally Zupka

Harvey and Janel Grossinger's family (Shirley's older son and family)

Mal and Linda Grossinger's family (Shirley's younger son and family)

ACKNOWLEDGMENTS

Kathy Shapiro drove me to meet her friend and that was how I was introduced to Margaret Osburn, a professional writer and editor who teaches memoir writing at Johns Hopkins. That was also when I began a careful survey of notes and chapters I'd developed over the years with the wish of sharing a special childhood and the need to focus and clarify what I had written. Kathy knew what she was about in sharing her friend and editor with me. Over two years, Margaret and I worked closely together, starting as editor and writer before establishing an enduring friendship.

Mike Bowler, retired education editor of *The Baltimore Sun,* read much of my writing. He critiqued and urged me on. Even during his last months of fading life from pancreatic cancer, Mike's encouragement and good humor remained. He and his wife Margaret were there from the beginning when I first thought there was a story to tell.

Linda Weisfeldt, a dear friend, has a folder that contains all the versions of this memoir. She too read, absorbed, and analyzed my stories. Her unflagging encouragement and suggestions buoyed me along. Many others who also read fragments, wrote to me, encouraged me, and shared their own experiences. Especially crucial to my narrative were the insights I gathered from the parents whom I counseled. Some had maintained contact over the years through my retirement as a social worker and when I served as a board member for the Hearing and Speech Agency in Baltimore.

My grandchildren have seen some of this memoir. Their interest and critical appraisals have been enormously helpful. Their willingness to take time from their busy lives has my gratitude. And then there are all my deaf relatives who, every summer and through messages during the year, speak of the past, of growing up under the influence of my parents, of their challenges and accomplishments. We especially enjoy our reunions at our home in Rehoboth every year. It has been during those times that we talked about what my experiences have been.

Some grandchildren were specific in their help. Tom Moses, a son-in-law, was always available at a time when the intricacies of my computer baffled me and came to my rescue. Tom Mandel, a grandson, brought his advertising reading skills forward when I got stuck and his wife, Johna, was the artist-cartoonist who assisted in developing the image for the book cover.

I appreciate their patience and rising to my side as needed.

My children—Sarah, Susan, Beth, and Barbara—have heard my stories. Sue arranged for a videographer to film and publish histories of both my husband and me to cement for our grandchildren a past in which they were not present. Beth read closely as I wrote, editing as I went along. Firstborn Sarah drew insights from my childhood. The youngest, Barbara, who maintained close contact with my mother—who moved to Baltimore at age ninety-five—experienced from her the telling and retelling of a life with challenges and purpose. I knew that the enveloping love and support they provided freed me as I pursued this project.

My husband, Bob, has been a part of my life since my childhood. He knows all the stories. He has loving connections with the individuals. In spite of his parents' insistence that he not, he married the girl with two deaf sisters.

The beloved scholar, Abraham Joshua Heschel, once stated, on linking the generations, that "The authentic individual is neither an end or a beginning but a link between ages, both memory and expectation. . . . Recollection is a holy act; we sanctify the present by remembering the past."

ABOUT THE AUTHOR

Miriam (Scharfman) Zadek is a recipient of the Maryland Governor's Service Lifetime Achievement Award, given in recognition of her forty-plus years of service to individuals and families facing communication challenges. She was hired by the Hearing and Speech Agency (HASA) of Metropolitan Baltimore in 1975 to develop a model of social work counseling for parents and families seeking communication access resources. Miriam is the founder of Maryland's only nonprofit American Sign Language interpreting referral agency, The Miriam Zadek Centralized Interpreter Referral Service and the Zadek Family Education Program, which provides opportunities for families and professionals to learn together in an interactive, inclusive environment.

Following her retirement in 1994, Miriam was asked to serve on the HASA board. During her twenty-five years as a board member (1995–2019), she obtained funding for the Gateway School's Frances Scholarship Endowment Fund, devoted to the benefit of critical early intervention and educational services. With a federal grant, she developed a model of intervention for families who have children with communication disorders. She authored booklets for parents with limited literacy, and the booklets were distributed through the Federal First Chance network. She also participated in a Gallaudet University group charged with developing learning materials for deaf persons with limited vocabulary. Upon retiring from the HASA Board of Directors, Miriam was appointed to the HASA President's Advisory Board.

Miriam, a graduate of Barnard College, earned a master's degree at Columbia University School of Social Work, where there is now an endowed Miriam Zadek scholarship for graduate students devoted to providing social work services to deaf and disabled people. She also earned certification from Gallaudet University in the counseling of persons experiencing hearing issues as adults.

Miriam is married to Dr. Robert Zadek, her high school senior prom date. The two reconnected during college and have been married for seventy years. They have four daughters, eleven grandchildren, and six great-grandchildren.